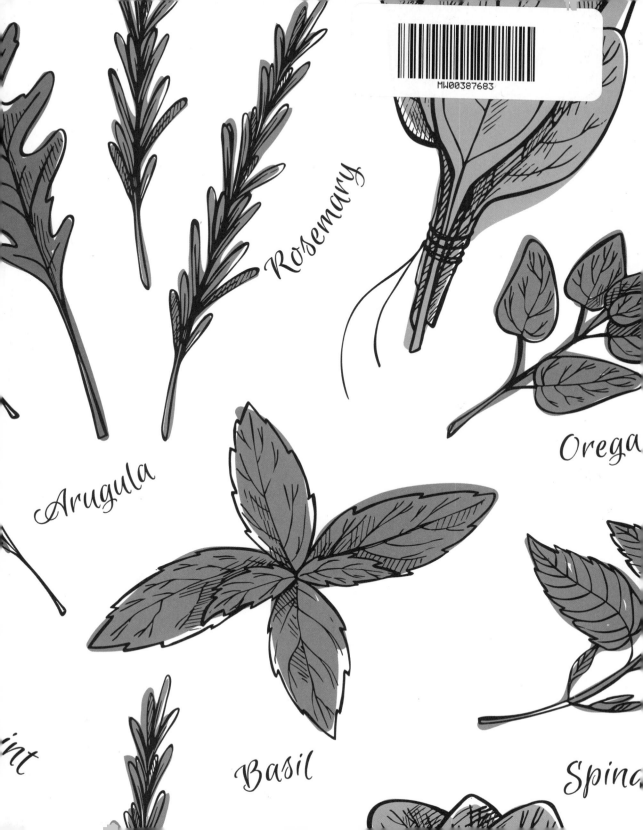

Rosemary

Arugula

Orega

Basil

Spina

int

Roast · Saute · Slow Cook · Steam · Sous Vide · Yogurt · Rice · Bake

MULTICOOKER
C O O K B O O K

Over
-220-
recipes and
photos!

In the
KITCHEN

Roast • Sauté • Slow Cook • Steam • Sous Vide • Yogurt • Rice • Bake

MULTICOOKER
C O O K B O O K

Over
-220-
recipes and
photos!

In the
KITCHEN

ALLISON WAGGONER

NATIONAL TELEVISION HOST, CHEF, AND AUTHOR OF THE
IN THE KITCHEN SERIES: *A COLLECTION OF HOME & FAMILY MEMORIES,
A GATHERING OF FRIENDS,* AND THE *AIR FRYER COOKBOOK*

FRONT TABLE BOOKS | AN IMPRINT OF CEDAR FORT, INC. | SPRINGVILLE, UTAH

ISBN: 978-1-4621-1917-2

Published by Front Table Books, an imprint of Cedar Fort, Inc.
2373 W. 700 S., Springville, UT, 84663
Distributed by Cedar Fort, Inc., www.cedarfort.com

LIBRARY OF CONGRESS CATALOGING-IN-PUBLICATION DATA

Names: Waggoner, Allison, 1966- author.
Title: In the kitchen. Multicooker cookbook / Allison Waggoner.
Other titles: Multicooker cookbook | Multi cooker cookbook
Description: Springville, Utah : Front Table Books, an imprint of Cedar Fort, Inc., [2016] | Includes index.
Identifiers: LCCN 2016030261 (print) | LCCN 2016030660 (ebook) | ISBN 9781462119172 (hardback : alk. paper) | ISBN 9781462126989 (epub, pdf, mobi)
Subjects: LCSH: Electric cooking. | Baking.
Classification: LCC TX827 .W34 2016 (print) | LCC TX827 (ebook) | DDC 641.5/884--dc23
LC record available at https://lccn.loc.gov/2016030261

Cover and page design by M. Shaun McMurdie
Cover design © 2016 Cedar Fort, Inc.
Edited by Justin Greer

Printed in the United States of America

10 9 8 7 6 5 4 3 2 1

www.cedarfort.com

To Bonnie's angel here on earth.

Food creates extraordinary moments for you and your family. There are great moments in our lives that happen when we break bread together. So raise your glass, try something new, call your mom, stay authentic, be thankful, and give someone a hug.

Thank you for sharing a little of your love for food with me.

Allison Waggoner

Contents

Introduction

Imagine the possibilities of one kitchen appliance versatile enough to cook in over 11 different cooking methods.

Welcome to the Multicooker!

A multicooker simply is a one-stop cooking pot which can roast, sauté, slow cook, steam, stew, sous vide, make yogurt, cook rice, and last but not least, bake!

In a multicooker, you can brown your meats, locking in the succulent flavors, sauté your ingredients, creating the delicious caramelized flavor. Then, simply switch to slow cooking, capturing intense and concentrated flavors that only extended slow cook times can deliver.

Not only can you have the ease of leaving sumptuous savory meals to cook all day, but imagine baking decadent cakes and breads to surprise and delight, or making tempting breakfast treats that nobody can resist.

The flexibility of the multicooker, together with over 220 recipes and photos included in this book, will surprise and inspire you to create enticing new menus.

The following pages provide guidance for enjoying the full potential of your multicooker. Learn how to make your old family favorites more flavorful and with fewer steps. Find easy to follow recipes to create yummy specialized dishes or learn to make your own Greek yogurt!

Step into the world of multicooking, and together with these exhilarating new recipes, be galvanized into the next generation of one-stop cooking pot deliciousness.

Frequently asked questions about multicookers

What size multicooker should I buy?

Multicookers come in many sizes and shapes. Cooking pots can vary from a small 1-quart size to the large 8-quart capacity. Cooking for a large group or family is best suited for using the 8-quart capacity. The 1-quart size is adequate for making small meals or a meal for one. Most recipes found in this book are best suited for a 5–6 quart size cooking pot, but tips to accommodate various pots can be found in the recipes—or read below for more information cook times or how much liquid to use.

Does it matter if my multicooker is round, square, or oval?

Depending on the make and model of your multicooker, the cooking pot shape can vary. All of the recipes included in this book can be cooked in whatever shape of cooking pot you own. Just note that your final result may have a different look than shown in the recipe photo, but the flavor and effect will still be the same. Each recipe provides clues on how to evaluate completed cook time, so use these for best results.

What's the difference between a four-hour or a six-hour cook time?

In many recipes, the cook time can vary with a 2-hour window. This is to accommodate the variances in types of multicookers on the market. If your cooker has higher wattage, or is smaller in size, cook time will be less. If using a larger capacity pot, or with less wattage, your cook time may be longer. Refer to each recipe for specific guidance on evaluating when your dish is finally ready.

When do I use the "High" or "Low" setting?

Experience shows to use the Low setting as much as you can, as this really allows the development of full flavor; plus, you can set the cooker in the morning, leave for the day and come home to wonderful, flavorful, cooked family meals. Individual recipes provide cooking information for either High or Low cook time. The general rule is that the High cook time should be doubled for Low cook time. For example, 1 hour on High = 2 hours on "Low." Additionally, multicookers have a higher-heat "Brown, Sauté, or Sear" setting. Use this setting as indicated in the recipes but rarely for longer cooking times.

One note to mention, if switching from High to Low when baking. Baking requires the high temperature to achieve results. Never substitute the High setting with the Low setting when baking breads, cakes, and other "baked" items.

How much liquid should I look for during cooking time?

Follow the direction for each recipe, and although some recipes will seem low on liquid, the liquid in the food will be sufficient. A general guide is to always maintain at least ¼ level of liquid in the cooking pot, and never increase over ¾ level of pot capacity. The recipe will indicate how much liquid is needed, and how to accommodate if using a smaller or larger pot.

Do I need to keep the lid on or off when cooking?

When using a multicooker on a higher heat or browning-type setting, you will be attending to the contents, so the lid will mainly be off. As you switch to a slow cooking function, you generally keep the pot covered. It is tempting to keep checking on the cooking food. Resist removing the lid too many times. Each time the lid is removed, valuable heat, steam, liquid, and flavor can escape. Certain recipes will indicate if cracking the pot lid is beneficial.

When baking in the pot, some recipes will call for a technique to prevent too much condensation building in the lid, causing soggy food results. This technique specifically calls for a paper towel, rather than dish or linen cloths. The paper towel is laid on the top of the cooking pot, directly underneath the lid, and it is never laid on or touches the food. The paper towel absorbs the collecting condensation and prevents liquid dripping on your baking foods. If you assess there is still too much collecting condensation, crack the pot lid slightly to generally alleviate the buildup.

Do I need to use pot liners or nonstick sprays?

There are many products on the market claiming better cooking pot results when using pot liners or using a nonstick cooking spray. The recipes in this book, unless specifically indicated, were simply made in the cooking pot, with no additional sprays or liners. Some of the recipes will indicate using parchment paper, foil, or a liner. This is specifically for greater ease in removing your final cooked recipe and better presentation results. With that said, if you're comfortable using liners and cooking sprays, use at your own discretion.

Can I only use these recipes if I have a multicooker or will they work in my slow cooker?

Yes, all these recipes will work in any straightforward slow cooker. The steps in the following recipes indicate using general functions on a multicooker. However, you still can follow these steps by simply using a pan on your stove top to achieve the same results. Use any above points when evaluating size and shape of your slow cooker and follow tips in recipes for adapting cook times.

Rice & Grain Cook Guide

Cook perfect rice and grains every time in your multicooker!

Instead of pulling out a rice cooker, or taking up space on a stove top, create fluffy rice or great grain recipes while walking away, allowing your multicooker to do all the work!

Follow these simple guide lines to cook in your multicooker.

GRAINS	YIELD	LIQUID	GRAIN	OPTIONS	COOK TIME
Wild Rice	6 cups cooked	4 cups water or reduced-sodium broth	2 cups rinsed and drained	Finely chopped onions & garlic	Low heat setting, 3–4 hours
Brown Rice	6½ cups cooked	3⅔ cups water or reduced-sodium broth	2 cups	2 Tbsp. olive and 1–2 Tbsp. fresh herbs, cut	High heat setting, 3–4 hours
Bulgur Wheat	6 cups cooked	4 cups water or reduced-sodium broth	2 cups	Fresh mint and parsley, cut	Low heat setting, 1–2 hours
Quinoa	6 cups cooked	4 cups water or reduced-sodium broth	2 cups rinsed and drained	Finely chopped root vegetables	Low heat setting, 2–3 hours
Barley	6 cups cooked	6 cups water or reduced-sodium broth	1½ cups pearl barley	Finely chopped leek and garlic	Low heat setting 3–4 hours
Steel-Cut Oats	6 cups cooked	6 cups water	2 cups	Dried fruit pieces	Low heat setting, 4–5 hours

Fish and Aromatics Guide

For those summer evenings or cozy winter nights when spending hours in the kitchen seems undesirable, use your multicooker for all of your fish dish favorites.

Below are some great starting points, but if you follow the rule of aromatics, you can create fantastic multicooker originals that will be a hit every time.

Aromatic cooking uses the fresh cooking smells of your chosen ingredients to permeate your fish, infusing flavor and succulent taste.

Place your chosen fresh herbs loosely in the bottom of your cooking pot, creating a bed, place your favorite fish filet on top of the herbs and cover with a choice flavor blend. Top with a citrus slice and cover to cook. Follow this simple guide and learn to create your own originals.

STEP 1 CHOOSE THE FISH	STEP 2 CHOOSE AROMATICS	STEP 3 CHOOSE SPICE	STEP 4 TOP WITH CITRUS	STEP 5 COVER AND COOK
Salmon	fresh dill, fresh parsley, sliced red onions, sliced garlic	Herbes de Provence	fresh lemon slices	
Halibut	fresh parsley, fresh cilantro, whole scallions, sliced garlic, sliced ginger	Chili powder	fresh lime slices	
Cod	fresh parsley, fresh mint, fresh thyme, whole leeks, minced garlic	Lemon pepper	fresh lemon slices	Select Slow cook function, High setting and cook for 1–2 hours or until fish flakes apart
Catfish	fresh dill, fresh rosemary, sliced shallots, sliced garlic	Salt and pepper	fresh tangerine slices	
Tilapia	fresh parsley, fresh lemon grass, whole scallions, minced garlic	Herbes de Provence	fresh ruby grapefruit slices	

Vegetable Roasting Guide

Instead of preheating or taking up space in your traditional oven, allow your multicooker to do the roasting while you step away from the kitchen for a while!

Use these roasted sides to compliment any of the recipes in this book. You may want to gently stir items to rotate them once or twice while cooking. Also add the flavors of fresh herbs while roasting. Adding a tablespoon of butter or olive oil will make your vegetables sing!

Follow these simple guide lines for roasting vegetables in your multicooker.

VEGETABLE	PREP	COOK TIME HIGH SETTING	COOK TIME LOW SETTING
2 lbs. potatoes	Peel, cut into 1" pieces	3-3½ hours	6–7 hours
2 lbs. zucchini (approx. 6 zucchini)	Half lengthwise and slice into 1" pieces	2–3 hours	4–6 hours
2 lbs. baby carrots	Peel, cut into 1" pieces	3-3½ hours	6–7 hours
2 lbs. broccoli	Cut into small florets	2–3 hours	4–6 hours
2 lbs. yellow squash (approx. 6 yellow squash)	Half lengthwise and slice into 1" pieces	2–3 hours	4–6 hours
2 lbs. green beans	Trim each end and cut into halves	2–3 hours	4–6 hours
2 lbs. parsnips	Peel, cut into 1" pieces	2–2½ hours	4–5 hours
2 lbs. cauliflower	Cut into small florets	2–3 hours	4–6 hours

Baking Guide

Your multicooker is a wonderful baker!

In the multicooker, bake cakes and make marmalades, jams, and even key lime pie!

Use this Baking Guide for great baking results every time. Remember that every multicooker will vary with size and wattage.

PROBLEM	CAUSE	SOLUTION
Cakes, rolls, and puddings come out soggy	Using slow cooking to bake causes higher amount of condensation, which collects on the lid and drips back onto your foods	Place paper (not cloth or linen) towel on the top of cooking pot directly under the lid. This will soak up the collecting condensation. Crack the lid if additional condensation collects
Some baked bases are browner in some spots.	Some cooking pots may have hotter heating areas	Most baking recipes call for using a liner. Use the liner to lift and turn the baked item during cooking time, allowing for even browning
Cakes and soufflés are dense and heavy.	The mix was cooked too low therefore not hot enough to cause the mix to rise and cook correctly	Never convert baking, bread making, or soufflé recipes to Low heat setting. These recipes need the High heat to allow for light spongy cake results
Jams, cakes, and pies seem too jiggly and loose.	Baked goods may need time to set up properly. The item may be undercooked.	Read directions to see if a "wait" or "cool" time is needed. If the item is not fully cooked, simply add cook time onto the recipe.

Breakfast, Butter & Jams

Vegetable Omelette Bake

6 eggs

½ cup milk

⅛ teaspoon garlic powder

⅛ teaspoon chili powder

1 cup broccoli florets

1 red bell pepper, thinly sliced

½ yellow onion, finely chopped

1 clove garlic, minced

1 cup shredded cheddar cheese

2 tomatoes, chopped

fresh parsley

In a large mixing bowl, whisk together eggs, milk, garlic powder, and chili powder until well combined.

Add the broccoli florets, sliced peppers, onions, and garlic.

Add egg mix to cooking pot. Cover and cook on Brown/Sauté function for 2 hours, but begin checking on omelet after 1 hour 30 minutes. The omelet is done when eggs are set. Sprinkle with cheese and cover; let stand 2-3 minutes or until cheese is melted.

Sprinkle with tomatoes and parsley and serve warm.

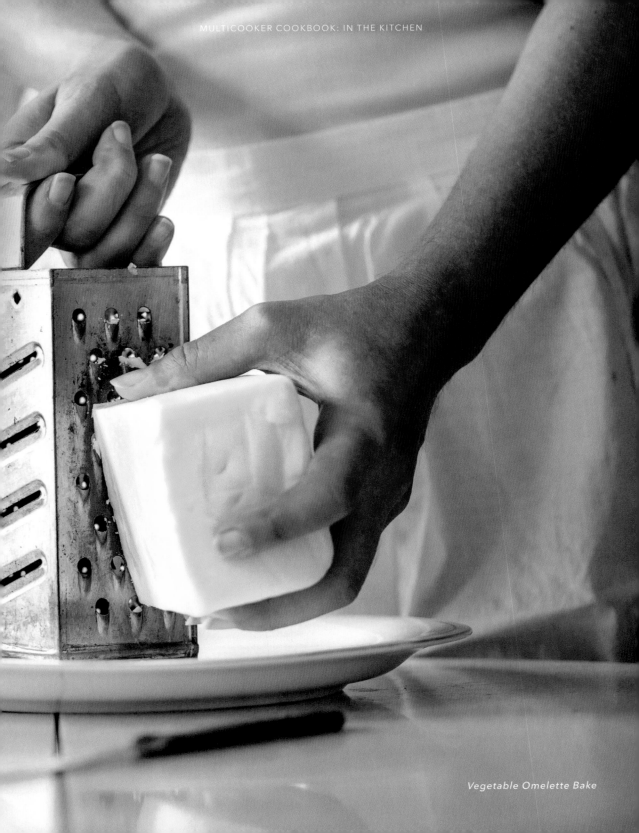

Vegetable Omelette Bake

Banana French Toast

Banana French Toast

1 12-inch baguette, sliced 1-inch thick

4 eggs

¾ cup whole milk

1 Tablespoon sugar

1 Tablespoon vanilla extract

1 teaspoon ground cinnamon

2 Tablespoons vegetable oil

2 bananas, sliced into rounds about ½-inch thick

½ cup pecan pieces

pure maple syrup

Place the baguette slices on the bottom of cooking pot.

Whisk together eggs, milk, sugar, vanilla, and cinnamon. Pour evenly over the baguette slices and stir gently to coat all the slices.

Arrange the banana slices atop the baguettes in the cooking pot. Drizzle with vegetable oil and sprinkle with the pecan pieces.

Cover and cook on Slow Cook function, High setting, for 2–3 hours or on Low for 4–5 hours, until cooked through. Cooking times can vary with different cookers, so cook until the bread begins to turn golden brown around the edges.

Lightly drizzle with maple syrup to serve.

Steel-Cut Oats with Cinnamon, Honey, and Vanilla Bean

2 cups water

1 cup whole milk

1 cup steel-cut oats

½ vanilla bean, halved and
  sliced lengthwise

1 cinnamon stick

1 teaspoon ground
  cinnamon

1 teaspoon honey

In the cooking pot, combine all ingredients and set to Slow Cook function, Low heat setting. Cover and let cook for 8–9 hours.

Remove the lid, then remove the vanilla bean and cinnamon stick and set aside. Stir in the ground cinnamon and honey to taste.

Add seasonal fruits to enjoy with your oats.

Steel Cut Oats with Cinnamon, Honey, and Vanilla Bean

Apple Butter

3 pounds apples, Granny Smith

2 (50-ounce) cans applesauce,
  unsweetened

4 cups sugar

1½ cups apple juice

2 teaspoons ground cinnamon

1 teaspoon ground cloves

1 teaspoon ground allspice

Peel, core and cut the apples into small pieces. Add all the ingredients into cooking pot and stir.

Cover and cook on Slow Cook function, Low setting, about 8–10 hours.

Remove the cover, stir, and taste. Continue cooking for a few more hours, uncovered, until some of the liquid is reduced and the butter has cooked down a bit.

Let cool and refrigerate.

Apple Butter

Cinnamon Rolls

Cinnamon Rolls

Dough

¾ cup whole milk

2½ teaspoons instant yeast

¼ cup + 1 teaspoon sugar

1 teaspoon salt

3 Tablespoons butter, room temperature

1 egg

2¾ cups all-purpose flour

Filling

5 Tablespoons butter, softened

1 Tablespoon ground cinnamon

⅓ cup granulated sugar

Icing

1¼ cups confectioner's sugar

2 Tablespoons maple syrup

2 Tablespoons whole milk

Dough

In a small saucepan, warm the milk over low heat until just warm.

In a large mixing bowl, add together the warmed milk, yeast, and 1 teaspoon sugar. Stir, then cover with a towel and let sit until the yeast begins to bubble, about 5–10 minutes.

With a hand mixer on low, beat into the milk mixture the remaining ¼ cup sugar, salt, butter, egg, and 2 cups of flour until well combined. The dough should be a bit sticky at this point.

Continue to beat on low speed and slowly add the remaining flour ¼ cup at a time until a soft dough forms. Dough will be ready when it gently pulls away from the side of the bowl. Let the dough rest for about 10 minutes.

While you let the dough rest, line your cooking pot with a piece of parchment paper that has been lightly sprayed with nonstick spray.

Filling

After 10 minutes, roll the dough out in a 14 × 8-inch rectangle. Evenly spread the softened butter on top. Sprinkle the cinnamon and sugar over the dough in an even layer.

Starting at one end, roll up the dough tightly into a long tube shape and then cut horizontally into 10–12 even pieces. Place them inside the lined cooking pot in a single layer.

This next step is crucial in making your rolls in a multicooker. Place a paper towel right under the lid of the cooking pot. This is important to help keep condensation off of the cooking rolls.

Set on Slow Cook function, High setting, and cook for 2¼ hours, or until the rolls are fully cooked through. Remove the rolls from the cooker right away by lifting out the parchment paper.

Icing

Whisk the confectioner's sugar, maple syrup, and milk together until smooth. Add a little more milk if icing is too thick. Drizzle over the warm rolls and serve.

Quick Breakfast Casserole

1 pound bacon

1 (32-ounce) bag frozen hash brown
  potatoes

½ red bell pepper, diced

½ green bell pepper, diced

8 ounces sharp cheddar cheese,
  shredded

12 eggs

1 cup milk

In cooking pot, brown bacon on Brown/Sauté function until crispy and brown. Remove and crumble the bacon. Keep 2 tablespoons of the bacon drippings in the bottom of the cooking pot and drain the rest.

Add half bag of hash browns to bottom of cooking pot. Add half of the crumbled bacon, onions, peppers, and cheese. Then layer the remaining hash browns, bacon, onions, peppers, and cheese.

In a medium-sized bowl, beat together the eggs and milk. Pour egg mixture over your casserole. Add salt and pepper on top to taste.

Cook on Slow Cook function, High setting, for 4 hours, or Low for 8 hours.

Quick Breakfast Casserole

Orange Marmalade

1¼ pounds Valencia oranges
4 cups water
juice of 1 meyer lemon
4 cups sugar

Wash, quarter, and seed the oranges, separating the peel from the pulpy center and cutting the peel into very thin slices. Transfer the orange pulp and peel to the cooking pot and add the water and lemon juice. Cover and cook on Slow Cook function on Low setting until simmering, about 2 hours.

Add the sugar and mix well. Stir often until you are sure the sugar has dissolved. This may take 5–10 minutes.

Continue cooking on Low setting for 6 hours, stirring every 2 hours to check for consistency. The peel will be translucent when the marmalade is ready for the next step.

Remove the lid, turn the cooker to Slow Cook function on High, and cook for another 2–3 hours.

Ladle the warm marmalade into clean glass jars and let stand until cool. Store, covered, in the refrigerator for up to 2 months.

Orange Marmalade

Meyer Lemon & Blueberry French Toast

Meyer Lemon & Blueberry French Toast

6 croissants, sliced in half lengthwise and toasted

½ cup blueberries

6 eggs, lightly beaten

2 cups half and half

2 Tablespoons vanilla extract

3 Tablespoons lemon zest

½ cup brown sugar

In the cooking pot arrange half of the bottom slices of the croissants in a single layer. Add the blueberries (or chosen fruit), spreading them over the first layer of croissants. Top fruit with the top slices of the croissants in a single layer.

In a bowl, whisk together the eggs, half and half, vanilla, lemon zest, and brown sugar until combined. Carefully pour the mixture over the bread in the cooking pot. Push down the bread/egg mixture. Take a piece of plastic wrap and cover the bread mix, pressing down slightly to remove any air bubbles from the top.

Place in the refrigerator for at least 2 hours, preferably overnight.

Remove plastic wrap, cover and cook on Slow cook function, High setting, for 2-3 hours or on Low for 4-5 hours, until cooked through.

Transfer to serving dish and serve immediately. Drizzle with Lemon Thyme Maple Syrup, below.

Lemon Thyme Maple Syrup

2 cups maple syrup

1 sprig fresh thyme

1 Tablespoon lemon zest

In a saucepan on your stovetop, pour in the 2 cups maple syrup. Add the sprig of thyme and lemon zest, and stir. Simmer over low heat for at least 30 minutes, stirring occasionally.

Drizzle the warm syrup over Meyer Lemon and Blueberry Toast.

Sausage and Sweet Pepper Hash

1 pound pork sausage, ground

1½ cups sweet onions, sliced

1½ pounds red potatoes, cut into ½-inch cubes

2 teaspoons fresh thyme

½ teaspoon ground black pepper

¼ cup chicken broth

½ cup red bell pepper, chopped to ½-inch pieces

½ cup green pepper, chopped to ½-inch pieces

½ cup yellow bell pepper, chopped to ½-inch pieces

½ cup Swiss cheese, shredded

2 teaspoons tarragon

In cooking pot on Brown/Sauté function, brown sausage meat. Add onion; cook until tender and just starting to brown, stirring occasionally.

Add in the potatoes, thyme, and black pepper. Pour broth over mixture in pot. Cover and cook on Slow Cook function, Low setting, for 5–6 hours or on High, about 2½–3 hours.

Stir in sweet peppers, sprinkle with cheese, and top with tarragon.

Sausage and Sweet Pepper Hash

Sweet Pumpkin Butter

Sweet Pumpkin Butter

2 cups pumpkin purée

1¼ cups maple syrup

1 teaspoon vanilla extract

2 teaspoons cinnamon

1 teaspoon ground ginger

½ teaspoon ground nutmeg

In the cooking pot, mix together pumpkin, maple syrup, and vanilla until smooth.

Cover, and cook on Slow Cook function, High setting, for 4 hours, or Low for 8 hours.

In the last hour of cooking, add the cinnamon, ginger, and nutmeg, and crack the lid to let moisture out if you want a thicker consistency.

Cool and store in jars at the bottom of your fridge.

Sausage Gravy and Biscuits

1 pound pork sausage

3 teaspoons flour

2½ cups whole milk

1 can biscuit dough, cooked as directed on package

In the cooking pot, brown sausage on Brown/ Sauté function until browned and cooked through. Stir in the flour and cook for 4-6 minutes.

Add milk and stir until desired thickness of gravy is reached. Add salt and pepper to taste.

Place cooked biscuits on top of the gravy and cover. Make sure the lid is slightly off center to allow steam to escape.

Keep gravy warm on Warm function for up to 4 hours. If gravy becomes too thick over time, add a little milk.

Sausage Gravy and Biscuits

Decadent Vanilla Bean Yogurt

Decadent Vanilla Bean Yogurt

1 gallon 2% milk

3 Tablespoons powdered milk

1 vanilla bean, sliced lengthwise

½ cup yogurt, with active cultures

1 Tablespoon vanilla extract

You will need a kitchen thermometer for successful results.

In the cooking pot add milk, powdered milk, then scrape in vanilla bean.

Set to Slow Cook function on Low setting, leaving the lid off. Use a thermometer for this process, as you need be precise when making yogurt.

Heat to 180 degrees. After reaching temperature, remove cooking pot and let cool to 100–110 degrees. Do not let the temperature drop below 90 degrees.

Stir in the yogurt and extract until it is smooth with no lumps.

Place the lid on the cooking pot and add pot back to the multicooker. Press the yogurt button and press start. Do not move the cooker once the function has started. The preset time is 8 hours.

You can add time if you would like it to be more tart, or more of a Greek style of yogurt. You can time this for up to 24 hours.

Once your yogurt is ready, move to the refrigerator for up to 7 days.

Peaches & Cream Steel-Cut Oats

1 cup steel-cut oats	4 cups water
1 cup dried peaches	½ cup half and half

In the cooking pot, combine all ingredients.

Set to Slow Cook function, Low heat setting. Cover and let cook for 8–9 hours.

Stir and serve in bowls.

Peaches & Cream Steel-Cut Oats

Ham & Brie Breakfast Casserole

Ham & Brie Breakfast Casserole

4 eggs

3 cups whole milk

2 cloves garlic, finely chopped

1 teaspoon fresh thyme, chopped

¼ teaspoon ground black pepper

6 cups French bread, cubed into
 1-inch cubes

1½ cups cooked ham, cubed into
 ¼-inch cubes

4 ounces brie cheese, cut into
 ½-inch pieces

¼ cup sun-dried tomatoes, thinly
 sliced

In the cooking pot, whisk together eggs, milk, garlic, thyme, and pepper.

Gently stir in bread cubes, ham, brie, and dried tomatoes.

Cover and cook on Slow Cook function, Low setting for 3½ – 4 hours or until a
knife inserted in center comes out clean.

Let stand covered for 30 minutes before serving.

Cinnamon Brioche Bread Pudding with Orange Zest Whipped Cream

Cinnamon Brioche Bread Pudding

Custard

¾ cup whole milk

¾ cup heavy cream

½ cup sugar

1 teaspoon vanilla extract

1 pinch nutmeg

1 teaspoon cinnamon

3 large eggs

Bread, Filling

3 ounces butter, softened

2 teaspoons sugar

2 teaspoons cinnamon

8 slices brioche, toasted until light brown

½ cup pecans, chopped

Custard

Combine the milk, heavy cream, sugar, vanilla extract, nutmeg, and 1 teaspoon of cinnamon in large bowl. Stir until the sugar is dissolved. Add the eggs and whisk until mixed completely.

Bread Filling

Mix the softened butter with sugar and cinnamon. Spread the mixture on each slice of bread. Cut the slices into 2-inch cubes, keeping 3 slices cut in half for the top if desired.

Assembly

Place the bread into the cooking pot. Top with half slices. Top with the pecans. Pour the milk mixture over the bread and press down to help the bread absorb the milk mixture. Let sit for 20 minutes.

Cover and cook on Slow Cook function, High setting for 2–3 hours or Low for 4–5 hours, until cooked through. Cooking times can vary with different cookers, so cook until the bread begins to turn golden brown around the edges.

Top the bread pudding with Orange Zest Whipped Cream recipe, below, and serve warm.

Orange Zest Whipped Cream

1 cup heavy cream

½ teaspoon vanilla extract

3 teaspoons orange zest

In a bowl, add cream and use an electric mixer to beat the cream on low until soft peaks start to form.

Add in vanilla and orange zest, mix until blended.

Serve on top of Cinnamon Brioche Bread Pudding.

Savory Onion Jam

6 large Red or Spanish onions
4 Tablespoons sugar
¼ cup balsamic vinegar
1 Tablespoon olive oil

Cut onions in half lengthwise; peel. Cut off ends; cut lengthwise into ¼-inch-thick pieces.

Set cooking pot on Brown/Saute function and heat oil. Add onions and cook, stirring occasionally until softened and translucent, about 6 minutes.

Add sugar, vinegar, ½ cup water and bring to a boil stirring with a wooden spoon.

Continue to cook, uncovered until liquid is syrupy, about 3½–4 hours. Transfer to a food processor; pulse until onions are coarsely chopped. Let cool, then refrigerate in airtight containers for up to 4 weeks.

Savory Onion Jam

Fruit and Nut Granola

⅔ cup honey

⅓ cup butter

½ cup chunky peanut butter

2 teaspoons ground cinnamon

1 Tablespoon vanilla extract

5 cups old-fashioned rolled oats

¼ cup pecans, chopped

¼ cup almonds, sliced

2 Tablespoons pumpkin seeds

2 Tablespoons sunflower seeds

¼ teaspoon salt

1 cup raisins

In cooking pot, combine the honey, butter, peanut butter, cinnamon, and vanilla. Turn temperature to Brown/Sauté function, allowing everything to melt together and combine smoothly.

Pour the oats, pecans, almonds, pumpkin and sunflower seeds, and salt into the cooking pot and coat thoroughly with honey mixture.

Place the lid onto the pot, leaving it slightly vented. Cook on Slow Cook function, High setting, for about 2 hours, stirring every 30 minutes.

Stir in the raisins right at the end. Spread the granola across a large baking sheet to let it cool before transferring to an airtight container.

Fruit and Nut Granola

Plat Du

— Soupe mino

*

— Pot au feu ave
à moëlle

Soups
&
Stews

Pork and Ginger Ramen

Pork and Ginger Ramen

3 pounds pork shoulder, cut into equal pieces that are 3–4 inches thick

1 yellow onion, chopped

6 cloves garlic, chopped

5 Tablespoons fresh ginger, peeled and chopped

1 leek, halved, cleaned, and chopped

½ pound button mushrooms, brushed clean and coarsely sliced

6 cups chicken broth

2 cups beef broth

1½ cups fresh ramen noodles

Toppings for Soup

4 eggs, soft boiled

bean sprouts, to taste

4 green onions, finely sliced

sesame oil, to taste

chili oil, to taste

soy sauce, to taste

Season pork with salt and pepper. Heat cooking pot on Brown/Sauté function and brown the pork on each side. Transfer to a plate and set aside.

Add the yellow onion and stir until browned, about 5 minutes. Stir in the garlic, ginger, leek, mushrooms, and broths. Stir to combine. Add back in pork.

Cover and set to Slow Cook function on Low setting for 8 hours.

Transfer the pork to a cutting board. Using two forks, break the pork into bite-size chunks. Using a large spoon, skim off and discard any fat from the surface of the broth. Return the pork to the cooking pot. Cover and warm on the Brown/Sauté function until warmed through.

Cook the ramen noodles according to the package directions. Divide the noodles evenly among individual bowls. Ladle the broth and pork over the noodles, dividing them evenly.

Toppings for Soup

Top each bowl with halved soft-boiled egg, bean sprouts, green onion, sesame and chili oil, and soy sauce. Serve right away.

Black Bean Soup with Smoked Turkey

2 red onions

2 Tablespoons olive oil

3 carrots, cut into large chunks

4 cloves garlic, smashed

1 Tablespoon flour

1 pound dried black beans, rinsed and drained

1 smoked turkey, drumstick (1¾-2 pounds)

2 Tablespoons pickling spices, tied in cheesecloth

¾ teaspoon red pepper flakes

½ cup fresh cilantro, chopped

sour cream and/or lime wedges for garnish

Set aside ½ an onion and chop the rest.

Heat the olive oil in cooking pot on Brown/Sauté function. Add the chopped onions, carrots, garlic, flour and stir while cooking until slightly browned, about 5 minutes.

Add the beans, turkey drumstick, pickling-spice packet, red pepper flakes, and 8 cups water. Cover and cook on Slow Cook function, Low setting, for 6 hours.

Remove the drumstick and shred the meat. Remove about 2 cups beans from the cooking pot and blend until smooth.

Return the beans and turkey meat to the soup and stir to mix.

Mince the reserved ½ onion.

Ladle the soup into bowls and top with the cilantro and minced onion. Garnish with sour cream and lime wedges if desired.

Chicken Nacho Soup

1 Tablespoon tomato paste

1 (14½-ounce) can diced tomatoes

1 russet potato, peeled and diced

1 zucchini, cut into ¾-inch pieces

½ white onion, finely diced

1 jalapeño pepper, finely chopped

1 clove garlic, finely chopped

1 teaspoon dried oregano

½ teaspoon ground cumin

3 sprigs fresh cilantro

1 (15-ounce) can hominy, drained and rinsed

¾ cup tortilla chips, crushed, plus whole chips for topping

4 cups chicken broth

1½ pounds skinless boneless chicken breasts, cut into ¾-inch pieces

8 ounces American cheese, diced

½ cup milk

Combine the tomato paste, tomatoes, potato, zucchini, onion, jalapeño, garlic, oregano, cumin, cilantro, hominy, crushed tortilla chips, chicken broth, and 1 teaspoon salt. Stir to combine.

Cover and cook on Slow Cook function, Low setting, for 7½ hours. Add the chicken and cook 30 more minutes.

Combine the cheese and milk in a medium microwave-safe bowl; microwave, whisking occasionally, until melted and smooth, about 2 to 3 minutes.

To serve, fill each bowl with soup and top with tortilla chips, a dollop of the cheese sauce, and sliced jalapeños.

Minestrone Soup

Minestrone Soup

1 cup dried white kidney beans, rinsed

3 Tablespoons extra virgin olive oil

2 onions, finely chopped

4 carrots, peeled, finely chopped

6 garlic cloves, minced

1 (28-ounce) can whole peeled tomatoes

4 cups chicken broth

4 cups vegetable broth

3 cups water

2 cups basil, chopped

1 teaspoon dried oregano

2 medium zucchini, quartered and chopped into ½-inch pieces

1 bunch Swiss chard, stems removed and chopped

½ cup Anelli pasta

Parmesan cheese, freshly grated

In the cooking pot, on Brown/Sauté function, add the beans and cover with 1 inch water. Cook beans until they are just beginning to soften, about 20 minutes. Drain beans and set aside.

In cooking pot, heat 3 tablespoons oil on the Brown/Sauté function. Add onions and carrots and cook until softened, about 5 minutes. Stir in garlic and cook until fragrant, about 30 seconds.

Add tomatoes and juice and cook until most of the liquid is reduced and the pan is nearly dry, 8-12 minutes.

Stir in broths, water, ½ cup basil, and oregano and bring to boil. Add the beans back into the pot. Cover and cook on Slow Cook function on Low setting until beans are tender, 6-7 hours (or cook on High setting 5-6 hours).

Stir zucchini, chard, and pasta into cooking pot. Cover and cook on Brown/Sauté function until pasta is tender, about 20-30 minutes. Stir in remaining basil and top with Parmesan.

Salmon Chowder with Dill

1 pound red-skinned potatoes, diced
2 carrots, thinly sliced
2 stalks celery, thinly sliced
½ white onions, diced
2 cloves garlic, minced
12 sprigs dill, chopped
12 sprigs parsley
6 sprigs thyme
2 bay leaves
1 wide strip lemon zest
3 cups clam juice
1 pound salmon fillet
½ cup heavy cream
fresh chives, chopped

Put the potatoes, carrots, celery, onion, and garlic in cooking pot.

Add the dill, parsley, thyme, bay leaves, and lemon zest. Pour in the clam juice; cover and cook on Slow Cook function, High setting, about 4½ hours.

Season the salmon with salt and pepper to taste.

Stir the heavy cream into the vegetables in cooking pot, then partially submerge the salmon in the liquid. Cover and cook for 1 more hour.

Discard the herb stems; season the chowder with additional salt and pepper as needed. Serve topped with chives.

Pictured above: Andrew Zimmern

Split Pea Soup

Split Pea Soup

2 onions, chopped

1 celery stalk, minced

2 Tablespoons butter

3 garlic cloves, minced

¾ teaspoon thyme, dried

¾ teaspoon salt

¼ teaspoon red pepper flakes

7 cups water

1 pound green split peas, picked over and rinsed

1 pound ham steak, rind discarded, quartered

1 (12-ounce) package smoked ham hock

2 bay leaves

Add the onions, celery, butter, garlic, thyme, ¾ teaspoon salt, and pepper flakes into cooking pot on Brown/Sauté function and cook until soft, about 5 minutes.

Add water, peas, ham steak, ham hock, and bay leaves into cooking pot.

Cover and cook on Slow Cook function, Low setting, until peas are tender, about 8–9 hours.

Transfer ham steak pieces to plate. Discard ham hock and bay leaves.

Whisk soup vigorously until peas are broken down and soup thickens, about 30 seconds.

Shred ham steak into bite-size pieces and return to soup. Season with salt and pepper to taste.

Beef and Barley Soup

1¼ pounds boneless beef chuck

1 cup pearl barley

½ pound mushrooms, quartered

4 stalks celery, quartered

6 carrots, quartered

2 leeks, sliced (white and light green parts only)

1 sprig fresh thyme

4 cups beef broth

1 Tablespoon soy sauce

In your cooking pot, combine the beef, barley, mushrooms, celery, carrots, leeks, thyme, beef broth, and soy sauce.

Add 1 cup water and salt and pepper to taste. Cover and cook on Slow Cook function, Low setting, for 8 hours. Do not stir.

Spoon out the beef and transfer to bowl, let cool slightly, and slice into bite-size pieces. You can skim a bit of fat off if you choose.

If the soup is too thick, add a small amount of water.

Divide the soup among shallow bowls and top with the beef pieces. Serve hot.

Beef and Barley Soup

Fish and Shrimp Stew

Fish and Shrimp Stew

2 Tablespoons butter

1 red onion, finely chopped

½ fennel bulb, minced

1 leek, white and light green parts, minced

1 Tablespoon garlic, minced

3 Tablespoons flour

3 Tablespoons tomato paste

4 Tablespoons white wine

1 (12-ounce) bottle clam juice

1 (14-ounce) can whole tomatoes, with juice

½ teaspoon saffron threads

2 Tablespoons lemon juice

1 pound shrimp, peeled and deveined

1 pound cod, or any preferred white fish

In cooking pot, add butter, onion, fennel, leek, and garlic on Brown/Sauté function and cook until tender, about 5–8 minutes.

Stir in the flour and cook for another 3–5 minutes until incorporated.

Add the tomato paste, wine, clam juice, tomatoes, saffron threads, and lemon juice to the pot and stir to combine. Cover and cook on the Slow Cook function, Low setting, for 4 hours.

Uncover and add the shrimp and fish and stir to mix well.

Re-cover the cooker and cook on the Slow Cook function, Low setting, for 1 hour.

French Onion Soup

4 Tablespoons butter

6 large yellow onions, quartered and cut into ¼-inch-thick slices

2 teaspoons salt

1 teaspoon pepper

1 Tablespoon brown sugar

2 teaspoons fresh thyme, chopped

5 Tablespoons flour

¾ cup dry sherry

¼ cup soy sauce

2 pounds beef bones

4 cups beef broth

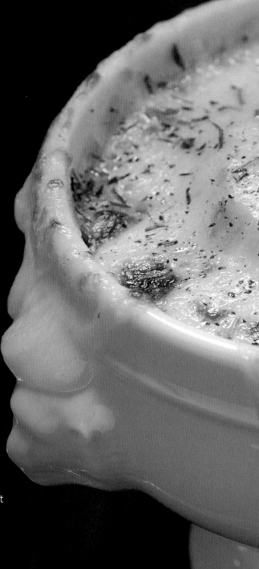

Heat cooking pot on Brown/Sauté function. Add butter, onions, salt and pepper, brown sugar, and thyme into the cooking pot. Sauté for 5 minutes.

In a small bowl, stir flour, sherry, and soy sauce together until smooth. Pour over onions in cooking pot and toss to coat.

Tuck bones under onion mix around edge of cooking pot.

Cover and cook on Slow Cook function, Low setting until onions are softened and deep golden brown, about 10–12 hours.

Remove bones from cooking pot. Add in beef broth and cook until beginning to boil.

Ladle soup into oven-ready bowls. Heat broiler. Add 2 croutons from recipe on following page. Top with Gruyère cheese. Broil until melted and bubbly, about 3–5 minutes.

Serve hot.

Croutons

2-3 Tablespoons olive oil
1 loaf French bread, cut into ½-inch slices

Preheat oven to 400 degrees.

Arrange bread slices in a single layer on baking sheet. Drizzle with olive oil and bake until bread is golden at edges, about 10 minutes.

To make herbed croutons for other dishes, such as salads: cut your bread into smaller cubes, place bread in bowl, and toss with olive oil. Add 1-2 Tablespoons of Parmesan cheese and your favorite herbs, such as rosemary or thyme. Arrange the bread as above and bake until indicated as above.

French Onion Soup

Wild Rice and Mushroom Soup

Wild Rice and Mushroom Soup

1 large onion, halved then thinly
  sliced

4 cloves garlic, minced

4 cups button mushrooms, sliced

1 cup shiitake mushrooms, sliced

2 cups cremini mushrooms, sliced

½ cup white wine

1½ cups vegetable stock

1 cup wild rice

3 Tablespoons cream

Add the onion, garlic, mushrooms, white wine, and stock to the cooking pot.

Cook on Slow Cook function, High setting for 2½ hours, stirring halfway through.

Once the vegetables are very soft, add rice and mix well. Cook on High for another 2 hours, or until the rice is fully cooked. Add additional broth as needed.

Add the cream and season to taste. Serve immediately.

White Tuscan Bean Soup

2 Tablespoons vegetable oil

6 ounces pancetta, chopped

3 onions, minced

8 cloves garlic, minced

¼ teaspoon salt

3 cups water

3 cups chicken broth

1 pound dried cannellini beans, rinsed, soaked overnight, and drained

2 bay leaves

½ teaspoon red pepper flakes

1 sprig fresh rosemary

Parmesan cheese, grated

Heat the oil in cooking pot on Brown/Sauté function. Add the pancetta and cook until golden, about 10 minutes. Stir in the onions, garlic, and salt and cook until the onions are softened and lightly browned, 10-15 minutes.

Stir in the water, broth, beans, bay leaves, and pepper flakes until combined.

Cover and cook on Slow Cook function, Low setting, until the beans are tender, 10-12 hours.

Add the rosemary sprig and continue to cook until lightly fragrant, about 15 minutes longer. Remove and discard the bay leaves and rosemary.

Season the soup with salt and pepper to taste and serve topped with Parmesan cheese.

White Tuscan Bean Soup

Pozole

Pozole

2 Tablespoons vegetable oil

1¼ pounds boneless pork shoulder, trimmed and cut into 4-inch pieces

1 medium white onion, chopped

5 garlic cloves, minced

1 teaspoon ancho pepper chili powder

1½ Tablespoons chili powder

4 cups chicken broth

2 Tablespoons cornstarch

4 Tablespoons cold water

1 (29-ounce) can hominy, drained and rinsed

1 avocado, cubed

2 limes, quartered

4 Tablespoons cilantro, chopped

Select Brown/Sauté function and add 1 Tablespoon oil to the cooking pot. Season pork with salt. Add the pork to the heated oil and cook until pieces are browned on all sides. When browned, remove to a large bowl.

Add additional 1 Tablespoon oil to the cooking pot. When hot, add the onion, garlic, and chili powders and sauté until soft, about 5 minutes. Add broth and return pork to cooking pot.

Cover and cook on Slow cook function, Low setting, for 6–7 hours, or on High for 4–5 hours, until the pork is tender.

Remove pork from cooking pot and use two forks to shred pork. Whisk together cornstarch and cold water; add to broth in cooking pot. Select Brown/Sauté function and stir until broth thickens. Stir in shredded pork and hominy. Season to taste with salt and pepper.

Serve with avocado, cilantro, and lime.

Pork Brisket Chili

1½ pounds boneless pork shoulder, cut into
  1-inch cubes

1½ pounds beef brisket, cut into 1-inch cubes

2 (15-ounce) cans kidney beans (do not drain)

1 (15-ounce) can diced tomatoes

1 red bell pepper, finely chopped

1 red onion, finely chopped, plus a little extra
  for topping

1 to 2 chipotle peppers in adobo sauce, finely
  chopped, plus 1 Tablespoon sauce from the
  can

2 Tablespoons chili powder

1 Tablespoon ground cumin

1 teaspoon dried oregano

1 teaspoon salt

Toppings

sour cream

grated Cheddar cheese

Season the pork and brisket with salt and
pepper to taste. Brown meat on each side on
Brown/Sauté function. Remove from pot and
set aside.

Combine the kidney beans and their liquid, the
tomatoes, bell pepper, red onion, chipotles and
adobo sauce, the chili powder, cumin, oregano,
and 1 teaspoon salt in cooking pot.

Add the pork and brisket and stir to combine.
Cover and cook on Slow Cook function, High
setting, for 8 hours. Season with additional salt
to taste.

Serve with cheese, sour cream, and extra red
onion toppings.

Pork Brisket Chili

Springtime Irish Stew

Springtime Irish Stew

3 pounds boneless lamb, shoulder, cut into 2-inch cubes

2 Tablespoons olive oil

1 Tablespoon butter

2 leeks, cleaned, white portion diced

1 fresh sprig thyme

1 fresh sprig rosemary

1 fresh bay leaf

2 cups beef broth

1 pound red potatoes

4 large carrots

1 cup frozen peas, thawed

2 Tablespoons apple cider vinegar

2 teaspoons dried dill weed

Pat the lamb dry with paper towels and season lightly all over with salt and pepper. In cooking pot, warm the oil on Brown/Sauté function. Working in batches, brown the meat on each side. Transfer to a plate.

Add the butter and leeks to the pot and cook, stirring occasionally, until softened, about 3 minutes. Add the thyme, rosemary, bay leaf, and broth to the pot.

Stir to combine and then return the meat and juices to the pot.

Cover and set to Slow Cook function on Low setting for 6 hours.

Meanwhile, cut the potatoes into quarters. Peel the carrots and cut them into chunks about the same thickness as the potatoes. Put the potatoes and the carrots on top.

Cover and set to Slow Cook function on Low setting for 2 hours.

Stir the peas, vinegar and dill into the pot.

Change setting to Brown/Sauté function bringing the stew to a simmer or until the peas are heated through, about 2–3 minutes.

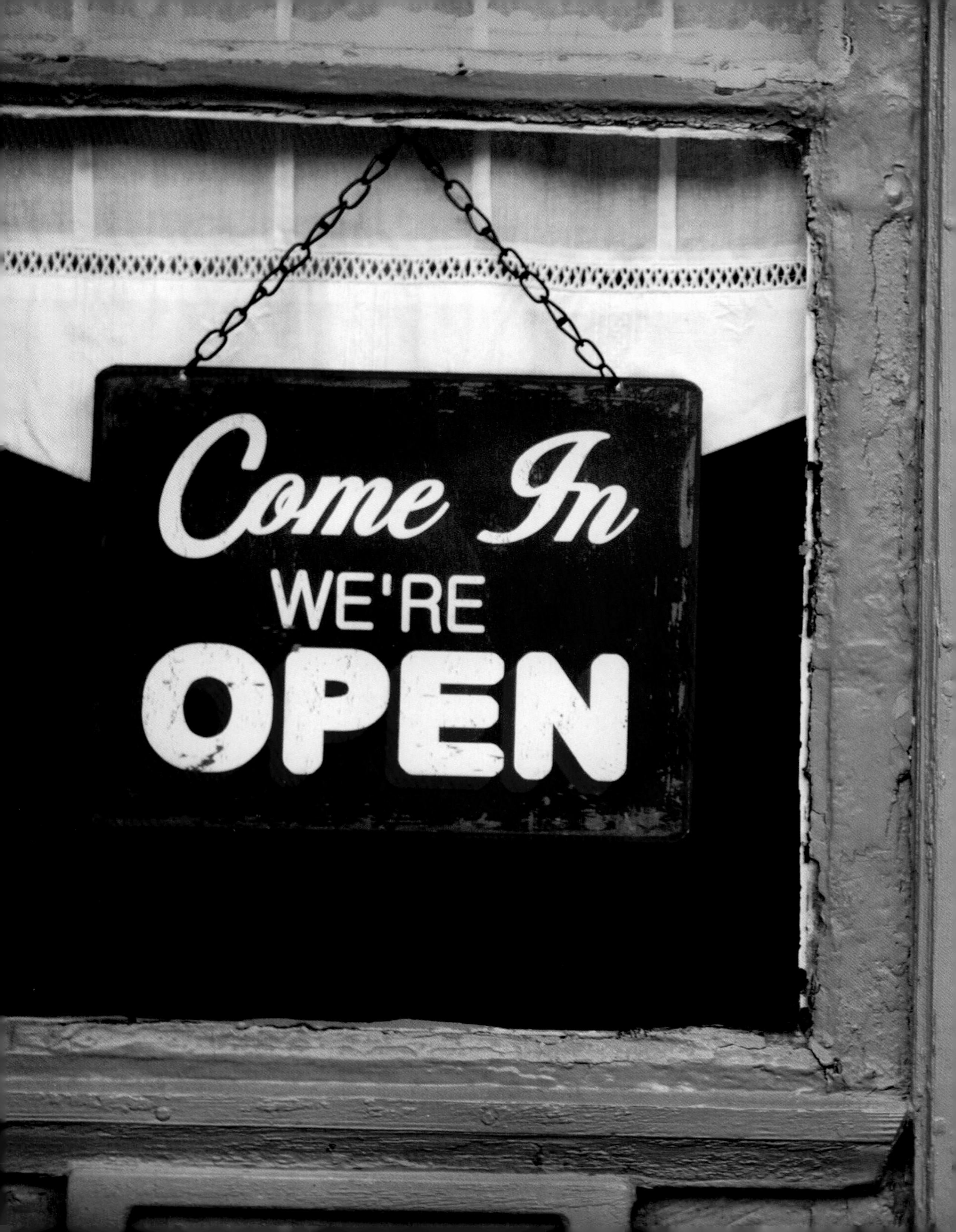
Come In
WE'RE
OPEN

Vegetables
& Sides

Beets with Lime and Toasted Pine Nuts

Beets with Lime and Toasted Pine Nuts

1½ pounds beets, whole (similar in size, 2–3 inches in diameter)

1¼ cups water

3 Tablespoons white vinegar

1 Tablespoon brown sugar

1 shallot, sliced thin or chopped

1 teaspoon lime zest

¾ cup roasted pine nuts

3 Tablespoons fresh cilantro , finely chopped

Scrub and trim the beets, leaving about one inch of the tops on and rootlets intact.

Place each beet on a square of foil and drizzle with about ½ teaspoon of olive oil; rub the oil over the surface of the beet. Bring the corners of the foil up around the beets and twist to seal. Repeat with the remaining beets.

Put the wrapped beets in the cooking pot, cover, and set on Slow Cook function on High setting for 3–4 hours, or until the beets are tender.

Remove beets from cooker and, when cool enough to handle, rub off skins with paper towel or dishtowel and cut into ½-inch wedges.

While beets are cooling, increase the heat to the Brown/Sauté function. Reduce the liquid by half cooking for 5–6 minutes. Add vinegar and sugar then return to boil and cook, stirring constantly with heat-resistant spatula, until spatula leaves wide trail when dragged through glaze, 1–2 minutes. Turn off heat.

Add beets, shallot, lime zest, and salt and pepper to taste. Toss in glaze to coat. Transfer beets to serving dish, sprinkle with pine nuts and cilantro, and serve.

Cornbread Pudding Casserole

12 ounces Cheddar cheese, shredded

12 ounces Monterey Jack cheese, shredded

2 (8½-ounce) packages cornbread mix

2 (10½-ounce) cans corn

2 (10½-ounce) cans creamed corn

2 cups sour cream

½ cup jalapeño chiles, pickled from jar and chopped

4 eggs, beaten

2 sticks butter, melted

1 cup milk

3 teaspoons sugar

2 teaspoons black pepper

1 teaspoon creole seasoning

In the cooking pot, mix 6 ounces of the Cheddar and 6 ounces of the Monterey Jack cheese together.

Add all the remaining items to the pot and stir to combine. (Keep the remaining cheese until later in the recipe.)

Cook on Slow Cook function on High setting for 3–4 hours depending on the size of your cooker.

For the last 30 minutes, uncover and top cornbread with the remaining cheese.

Cornbread Pudding Casserole

Balsamic Brussel Sprouts

Balsamic Brussel Sprouts

2 pounds brussel sprouts, trimmed
  and halved

2 Tablespoons olive oil

2 Tablespoons butter, cut into
  cubes

½ cup balsamic vinegar

2 Tablespoons brown sugar

4 ounces Parmesan cheese, shaved
  into large flakes

Place brussel sprouts into cooking pot. Stir in olive oil and season with salt and pepper to taste. Top with butter.

Cover and cook on Slow Cook Function, Low setting, for 3-4 hours, or High for 1-2 hours.

To make the balsamic reduction, add balsamic vinegar and brown sugar to a small saucepan over medium heat. Bring to a slight boil and reduce by half, about 6-8 minutes; set pot aside and let cool.

Drizzle brussel sprouts with balsamic reduction, top with Parmesan flakes, and serve immediately.

Green Bean Casserole

3 Tablespoons butter, salted

1½ pounds button mushrooms, sliced

1 yellow onion, diced

8 ounces cream cheese, room temperature

1 cup chicken stock

2 pounds green beans, rinsed and trimmed,
  cut into 1½-inch pieces

2 cups fried onions

In your cooking pot, heat the butter on Brown/Sauté function until it has just begun to brown.

Add the mushrooms for 7-10 minutes. Add the onion to the mushrooms. Continue to cook until the onions are translucent.

Put the cream cheese and chicken stock into the cooking pot, cover, and cook until the cheese has fully melted.

Add to the pot, the trimmed and rinsed green beans, stirring to coat all the beans. Cover and cook on Slow Cook function, Low setting, for 5 hours, or on High for about 2 hours. Stir again and top with the fried onions.

Green Bean Casserole

Robust Goat Cheese Mashed Potatoes

2 pounds russet potatoes, roughly
  cut into 1-inch cubes

3 cloves garlic, peeled

3 scallions

2 sprigs fresh thyme

1 cup chicken broth

¾ cup heavy cream

5 ounces goat cheese

1 teaspoon salt

½ teaspoon pepper

Place the potatoes, garlic, scallions, thyme sprigs and chicken broth in the cooking pot.

Cover and set to Slow Cook function, High setting, for 4–5 hours or until the potatoes are very tender and soft.

Drain the potatoes and place in a large mixing bowl. Discard the scallions and thyme sprig.

Add in the heavy cream, goat cheese, salt, and pepper and mash together. Serve hot.

Robust Goat Cheese Mashed Potato

Stuffed Red Peppers

Stuffed Red Peppers

4 red bell peppers

1½ cups chicken broth

¾ cup arborio rice

8 ounces hot or mild Italian sausage, bulk

1 onion, finely chopped

6 garlic cloves, crushed

½ teaspoon dried oregano

1 (28-ounce) can crushed tomatoes

1¼ cups Parmesan cheese, grated

2 Tablespoons basil, chopped

Clean the peppers, then cut the tops offs and discard the stems and seeds. Chop pepper tops into ¼-inch pieces and reserve the pepper cups.

Microwave broth and rice in covered large bowl until liquid is absorbed and rice is nearly tender, about 13–15 minutes.

In the cooking pot, cook sausage on the Brown/Sauté function until browned. Using slotted spoon, transfer sausage to paper towel–lined plate.

Pour off all but 1 tablespoon fat from the cooking pot and then add onion, chopped pepper tops, garlic, and oregano and cook for 3–5 minutes till softened and fragrant. Add tomatoes and bring to boil; turn off heat. Let peppers continue to cook slightly.

In a large bowl, combine 1 cup of the cooking pot sauce, browned sausage, 1 cup Parmesan cheese, and rice

Fill each pepper cup with one-quarter of rice mixture and place upright in cooking pot. Top pepper cups with remaining ¼ cup Parmesan cheese.

Cover and cook on Slow Cooker function, Low setting until peppers and rice are tender, about 4–4½ hours.

Sprinkle with basil and serve.

Parmesan Risotto

2 Tablespoons butter

1 onion, finely chopped

2 garlic cloves, minced

1½ cups arborio rice

½ cup white wine

2 Tablespoons cognac

4 cups chicken broth

¾ cup Parmesan cheese, grated

Heat cooking pot on Brown/Sauté function and melt butter. Add onion and cook until softened, about 5 minutes. Stir in garlic and cook another minute.

Stir in rice and toast lightly, about 3–5 minutes. Stir in wine and cognac and cook until almost evaporated, about 1 minute. Stir in 3¼ cups broth. (Keep remaining broth for use later if needed.)

Cook on Slow Cook function, High setting for 2-2½ hours. Stir in Parmesan cheese; cook uncovered until Parmesan cheese is melted, about 15 minutes.

At this point risotto still may look watery, but continue to stir. Change to Brown/Sauté function and stir for 5-7 minutes until liquid has become thickened. If it becomes too thick, add in remaining broth.

Parmesan Risotto

Entertaining & Sharing

Parmesan Ranch Oyster Crackers

2 (8-ounce) packages oyster crackers

1 (1-ounce) package ranch salad dressing mix

3 cloves garlic, minced

¼ teaspoon dried dill

¼ cup vegetable oil

¼ cup butter

½ cup Parmesan cheese, finely grated

Add oyster crackers, ranch seasoning, garlic, and dill. Stir in vegetable oil and gently toss to combine.

Cover and set on Slow Cook function, Low setting for 1 hour, stirring occasionally. Stir in butter until melted, about 1–2 minutes.

Remove crackers from cooking pot and place in a single layer onto a baking sheet. Stir in Parmesan and let cool completely.

Parmesan Ranch Oyster Crackers

ALLISON WAGGONER

Buffalo Chicken Dip

Buffalo Chicken Dip

1 (8-ounce) package cream cheese, cut into 8 slices

4 ounces blue cheese, crumbled

3 cups chicken, cooked and shredded

2 cups mozzarella cheese, shredded

1 cup hot sauce

1 cup sour cream

1 Tablespoon ranch salad dressing mix

4 scallions, sliced

Add all ingredients, except the scallions, to the cooking pot and stir until combined.

Cook on Slow Cook function, High setting, 1½–2 hours, or until the cheeses are all melted. Stir well.

Top with scallions and serve with chips or your desired dippers.

Hot Chipped Beef Dip

1 (8-ounce) package cream cheese, softened

1 (8-ounce) container sour cream

1 Tablespoon cream-style horseradish

2 (2.8-ounce) cans dried chipped beef

½ red onion, chopped

½ cup celery, chopped

2 teaspoons fresh dill, chopped

rye bread, toasted

In cooking pot, combine all ingredients, except the rye bread. Cover and cook on Slow Cook function, Low setting for 3 hours, stirring often.

Serve with slices of toasted rye bread.

Cheese Fondue

Cheese Fondue

3 cups chicken broth

3 cups heavy cream

1 cup white wine

3 garlic cloves

½ cup butter, room temperature

½ cup flour

16 ounces Emmentaler cheese, shredded

1 Tablespoon Dijon-style mustard

In cooking pot, combine the broth, cream, wine, and garlic. Cover and cook on Slow Cook function, Low setting, for 4–5 hours.

In a small bowl, mix the butter and flour together until it forms a paste. Add into broth mixture, stirring until combined. Cover and cook for 1 hour.

Slowly stir in cheese until smooth. Add in mustard and serve.

Suggested dippers: French bread, apples, vegetables.

Swedish Cocktail Meatballs

6 Tablespoons butter

2 onions, minced

4 slices caraway-rye bread, crusts removed, torn into pieces

2½ cups beef broth

1 cup chicken broth

1 cup sour cream

2 egg yolks

½ teaspoon ground allspice

¼ teaspoon ground nutmeg

½ teaspoon salt

½ teaspoon pepper

1 pound ground beef

1 pound ground pork

½ cup flour

2 Tablespoons soy sauce

In the cooking pot, melt 1 Tablespoon butter on Brown/Sauté Function. Cook onions until softened, about 6–10 minutes. Transfer to large bowl and let cool.

Add bread, ¼ cup broth, ¼ cup sour cream, yolks, allspice, nutmeg, salt, and pepper to bowl with onions and stir until combined and smooth. Add the beef and pork; knead with hands until well combined.

Form into ½-inch balls and set aside.

In cooking pot, melt remaining 5 tablespoons of butter on the Brown/Sauté Function. Whisk in flour and cook until beginning to brown, about 4–5 minutes.

Slowly stir in remaining broth and bring to boil. Set to the Slow Cook function, Low setting, and carefully add in meatballs. Cover and cook for 4½ hours.

Gently stir in the remaining ¾ cup sour cream and soy sauce.

We use a milk-and-bread panade to help keep our swedish meatballs tender. Rye bread flavored with caraway seeds gives these meatballs a Swedish-inspired flavor.

Swedish Cocktail Meatballs

ALLISON WAGGONER

Queso Blanco Cheese Dip

Queso Blanco Cheese Dip

2 Tablespoons cilantro
1 (4-ounce) can green chilis
½ Tablespoon jalapeño chiles
1 pound American cheese, shredded
1 Tablespoon butter
1 (8-ounce) package cream cheese
3 Tablespoons milk
2 tomatoes, finely chopped

Add all items into the cooking pot. Stir to combine.

Cover and set on Slow Cook function, Low setting, and cook for 2 hours. Serve with chips.

Spinach and Artichoke Dip

2 (14-ounce) cans artichoke hearts, drained and chopped

1 (10-ounce) package frozen spinach, thawed and squeezed dry

8 ounces sour cream

1 small onion, diced

2 cloves garlic, crushed

¾ cup grated Parmesan cheese

¾ cup milk

½ cup crumbled Feta cheese

⅓ cup mayonnaise

1 Tablespoon red wine vinegar

¼ teaspoon freshly ground black pepper

8 ounces cream cheese, cubed

Place artichoke hearts, spinach, sour cream, onion, garlic, Parmesan, milk, Feta, mayonnaise, vinegar, and pepper into the cooking pot.

Stir until well combined. Top with cream cheese.

Cover and cook on Slow Cook function, Low setting for 2 hours.

Uncover and stir until cream cheese is well combined. Cover and cook on Slow Cook function, High setting, for an additional 15 minutes.

Spinach and Artichoke Dip

Menù del
Pasta Giorno
Amatriciana

Petto di: Tacchino
al Forno
Patate Novelle
al Forno

€ 15,00

Pasta

Classic Bolognese Sauce

Classic Bolognese Sauce

3 Tablespoons butter

½ onion, finely chopped

1 carrot, peeled and finely chopped

1 rib celery, finely chopped

3 cloves garlic, minced

½ teaspoon pepper

3 Tablespoons tomato paste

1½ pounds ground pork

1½ pounds ground beef

1 teaspoon salt

3 cups whole milk

1½ cups red wine

3 cups dry white wine

2 (28-ounce) cans whole tomatoes, blended in blender or processor until smooth

½ teaspoon red pepper flakes

1 teaspoon fresh thyme leaves, chopped

Heat butter in cooking pot on Brown/Sauté function until melted and bubbling. Add onion, carrot, and celery and cook until softened, about 5–7 minutes. Add garlic and tomato paste and cook about 1 minute. Add meat, 1 teaspoon salt, and ½ teaspoon pepper and cook, breaking up meat, until crumbled into tiny pieces and lightly browned, about 5–8 minutes.

Add milk, bring to vigorous simmer, and cook until milk evaporates, about 10–15 minutes. Add wines, tomatoes, red pepper flakes, and thyme; cover and bring to boil.

Once mixture comes to boil, reduce to Slow Cooker function on Low setting and simmer until sauce is very thick, 7–8 hours. Season with salt and pepper and serve.

Baked Ziti

2 Tablespoons olive oil

½ pound sweet Italian sausage, bulk

½ pound hot Italian sausage, bulk

½ onion, chopped

4 garlic cloves, finely chopped

½ teaspoon dried oregano

½ teaspoon salt

½ teaspoon pepper

8 ounces ziti

1 (28-ounce) can diced tomatoes

1 (15½-ounce) can tomato sauce

8 ounces whole ricotta cheese

4 ounces mozzarella cheese, shredded

2 Tablespoons fresh basil, thinly sliced

In cooking pot, heat oil and brown the sausage for 6–8 minutes on Brown/Sauté function. Add onion, garlic, oregano, salt, and pepper. Combine and cook for another 2 minutes until fragrant.

Set to Slow Cook Function, Low setting, and add ziti, diced tomatoes, and tomato sauce. Cover and cook until pasta is tender, about 3 hours.

Drop ricotta in by spoonfuls over ziti and sprinkle with mozzarella. Cover and let sit for 20 minutes to let cheeses melt. Garnish with basil and serve.

Cheesy Tortellini

1 Tablespoon olive oil

1 pound ground beef

1 onion, diced

2 cloves garlic, minced

1 (28-ounce) can crushed tomato

1 (10-ounce) can diced tomatoes

½ teaspoon dried oregano

½ teaspoon dried basil

¼ teaspoon crushed red pepper flakes

1 (9-ounce) package refrigerated three-cheese tortellini

1 cup mozzarella cheese, shredded

½ cup Cheddar cheese, shredded

In cooking pot, heat olive on the Brown/Sauté Function. Add the ground beef, onion, and garlic. Cook until beef has browned, about 3-5 minutes; drain excess fat.

Add the crushed tomatoes, diced tomatoes with green chiles, oregano, basil, and red pepper flakes into the cooking pot. Stir until well combined.

Cover and cook on Slow Cook function, Low setting, for 7-8 hours, or High for 3-4 hours.

Uncover and stir in tortellini; top with cheeses. Cover and cook on Low setting for an additional 15-30 minutes, or until tender.

Spinach and Mushroom Lasagna

2 (15-ounce) packages ricotta
  cheese, whole milk

1 (10-ounce) package spinach,
  thawed and squeezed dry

8 ounces mushrooms, sliced

2 Tablespoons fresh basil

6 cups mozzarella cheese, whole
  milk, shredded

½ cup grated Parmesan cheese

1 (32-ounce) jar marinara sauce

12–18 lasagna noodles

Stir the ricotta, spinach, mushrooms, basil, and salt and pepper to taste in a large bowl. In a medium bowl, combine the mozzarella and Parmesan.

Spread about ½ cup marinara sauce in a thin layer in base of cooking pot. Cover with a single layer of uncooked lasagna noodles, breaking them as needed to fit. Spread one-third of the ricotta mixture over the noodles. Top with about one-third of the marinara sauce, then sprinkle with about one-third of the mozzarella mixture.

Repeat the layers (noodles, ricotta, marinara sauce, mozzarella mixture). Top with the remaining noodles, the remaining marinara, and the mozzarella mixture.

Cover and cook on Slow Cook function, Low setting, for 4 hours. Uncover and let rest 15 minutes so the excess liquid is absorbed.

Spinach and Mushroom Lasagna

Stuffed Shells with Spinach

Stuffed Shells with Spinach

1 cup frozen spinach, chopped, thawed, and squeezed dry

1 (12-ounce) ricotta cheese, whole milk

3 cups mozzarella cheese, shredded

4 ounces Parmesan cheese, grated

2 cloves garlic, minced

1 Tablespoon Italian seasoning

28 jumbo pasta shells

2 (24-fluid ounce) jars marinara sauce

In a large bowl, stir spinach, ricotta cheese, 2 cups mozzarella cheese, Parmesan, garlic, and Italian seasoning. Fill each pasta shell with the cheese mixture.

Add 3 cups marinara sauce to the bottom of the cooking pot and place half of the filled pasta shells. Cover with 2 cups of marinara sauce and top with remaining shells.

Cover and cook on the Slow Cook function, High setting, for 3-4 hours, or Low for 6-8 hours until shells are cooked.

Remove lid and sprinkle remaining 1 cup mozzarella cheese over shells. Wait 5 minutes until cheese is melted.

Spicy Chicken Linguine

1 pound boneless, skinless chicken breast, cut into ½ inch pieces

8 cups chicken broth

2 cups beef broth

¼ cup hot sauce

1 (8-ounce) can tomato sauce

¼ cup brown sugar

¼ teaspoon red pepper flakes

1 Tablespoon corn starch + 1 Tablespoon water, whisked together

¼–½ cup heavy cream

10 ounces linguine pasta noodles, uncooked

Place chicken in cooking pot.

In a large bowl, stir together the broths, hot sauce, tomato sauce, sugar, red pepper, and corn starch mixture. Add to the cooking pot with the chicken.

Cover and cook on the Slow Cook Function, High setting, for 3–4 hours, or Low for 6–8 hours.

Turn the cooker to Brown/Sauté function and add cream and noodles. Press noodles in liquid, stirring a few times. Bring liquid to a boil and return to the Slow Cook function, High setting. Continue to cook until noodles are done.

Spicy Chicken Linguine

Mac and Cheese

Mac and Cheese

8 ounces elbow macaroni, cooked

1 (12-ounce) can evaporated milk

1½ cups whole milk

¼ cup butter, melted

1 teaspoon salt

2 eggs, beaten

2 (10-ounce) packages bricks sharp Cheddar cheese, grated

dash of paprika

Mix in the cooking pot, the macaroni, evaporated milk, whole milk, butter, salt, pepper, eggs, and all but ½ cup of the grated cheese. Stir until combined.

Sprinkle the remaining ½ cup cheese over the top of the mixture, then sprinkle with paprika.

Cover and cook on Slow Cook function, Low setting, for 3¼ hours. Turn off the cooker and stir the mixture. Serve hot.

Lasagna Tower Stack

2 (9-ounce) packages lasagna noodles (use a premium brand of noodles or they will not hold up. We used Barilla's oven-ready 9-ounce box)

2 Tablespoons olive oil

1 (14¼-ounce) can canned whole tomatoes

2 pounds hot and mild beef sausages (use one pound each or all mild/hot)

3 teaspoons Italian seasoning

3 Tablespoons all-purpose flour

3 Tablespoons dry milk powder

1 eggplant, sliced on mandoline

1 zucchini, sliced lengthwise on mandoline

2 portobello mushrooms, caps sliced

4 ounces part-skim mozzarella, grated

2 cups spaghetti sauce (or prepared bolognese sauce) for serving

Put the noodles in a 9×13-inch dish with 2 tablespoons of olive oil. Pour enough hot water over to cover. Set aside for 20 minutes or until pliable. Drain the noodles, separate them, and set aside.

Depending on the size of your cooking pot, use 4–6 noodles to make a row around the inside walls, and then cover the bottom. Overlap the noodles slightly and press against the sides so they stick. On the sides, just do one row and you can add as you fill the pot up.

Crush ⅓ of tomatoes with your hand into the bottom, spread evenly over the top of the noodles. Cover with ⅓ of the sausage and then sprinkle over sausage 1 teaspoon of the Italian seasoning, 1 tablespoon of flour, and 1 tablespoon dry milk. Layer ⅓ of the eggplant, zucchini, and mushrooms in layers. Add ¼ of the remaining noodles in a layer, cut to fit any gaps, slightly overlapping the pieces. Gently press down on the noodles before building next layer.

Repeat the layers two more times starting with the tomatoes.

Spread the tomato juice from the can on the top of the last layer of noodles.

Set to Slow Cook function on Low setting for 4 hours, or until a knife easily slides through the layers. Turn off the cooker, top with the cheese, cover, and let sit for 20 minutes before serving.

Slice and serve with warmed bolognese sauce.

We made this in a round cooking pot, as pictured, but results will still be as effective in a square or oval cooking pot.

Lasagna Tower Stack

Plat du jour

Main Dishes

Balsamic and Honey Pulled Pork

Balsamic and Honey Pulled Pork

3 pounds boneless pork shoulder

½ cup chicken broth

1 yellow onion, chopped

½ teaspoon dried thyme

½ teaspoon dried rosemary

1 cup balsamic vinegar

¾ cup ketchup

⅓ cup honey

¼ cup dark brown sugar, packed

1 Tablespoon Worcestershire sauce

1 Tablespoon Dijon-style mustard

2 cloves garlic, minced

hamburger buns

coleslaw (optional)

Trim fat from pork roast then place roast in cooking pot and pour broth over top. Add the onions, thyme, and rosemary and lightly sprinkle with pepper.

Cover and set to Slow Cook function on Low setting for 8–10 hours, or on High for about 4½ hours.

During last 30 minutes of roast cooking, in a medium saucepan whisk together balsamic vinegar, ketchup, honey, brown sugar, Worcestershire, mustard, garlic, and salt and pepper to taste. Bring the sauce to a boil over medium heat, then reduce to a simmer and cook, stirring occasionally, until slightly thickened, about 20–25 minutes.

Remove pork from cooker, shred, and remove any excess fat. Drain onions and broth from cooker and discard. Return shredded pork to cooker; set cooker to Warm. Pour in balsamic sauce mixture and toss to evenly coat. Serve on buns with coleslaw as desired.

Rotisserie Chicken

1 (4–5 pound) whole chicken
1 Tablespoon smoked paprika
2 teaspoons salt
1 teaspoon black pepper
½ teaspoon garlic powder
¼ teaspoon onion powder
4 carrots, thickly sliced
4 celery stalks, thickly sliced
2 onions, thickly sliced

Rinse the chicken thoroughly and pat it dry with paper towels.

In a small bowl, combine the paprika, salt, pepper, garlic powder, and onion powder. Rub the seasoning mix all over chicken.

In the bottom of the cooking pot, place the carrots, celery, and onions. Place the chicken on top of the veggies.

Cover and cook on Slow Cook function, Low setting for 6-8 hours until it reaches the temperature of 160 degrees.

Rotisserie Chicken

Beef Tacos with Salsa Verde

Beef Tacos with Salsa Verde

1 Tablespoon vegetable oil

3 pounds beef chuck roast

½ teaspoon ground cumin

1 (16-ounce) jar salsa

½ white onion, chopped

2 cloves garlic, minced

½ cup chopped fresh cilantro

12 corn tortillas, warmed

4 radishes, sliced thin

3 lime wedges for serving

2 cups lettuce, shredded

1 tomato, chopped

1 avocado, sliced thin

Heat the vegetable oil in cooking pot on Brown/Sauté function. Season the beef with the cumin and salt and pepper to taste. Brown beef strips on both sides.

Add the salsa, onion and garlic. Cover and cook on Slow Cook function, High setting, for 6 hours.

Remove the meat to a cutting board and shred, discarding the excess fat. Return the meat to the cooking pot and stir in the cilantro.

Serve the meat in warmed tortillas, topped as desired with radishes, lime, lettuce, chopped tomato, and avocado slices.

Beer Brats

1 pound onions, sliced into ¼-inch-thick
  slices

¼ cup soy sauce

2 Tablespoons packed brown sugar

2½ pounds bratwurst (10 sausages)

3 cups dark beer

¼ cup hearty Dijon mustard, plus
  extra for serving

½ teaspoon caraway seeds

1 cup sauerkraut

10 hoagie rolls

In the cooking pot, combine onions,
soy sauce, and sugar and cook for 5–7
minutes on Brown/Sauté function until just
softened. Arrange bratwursts in single layer
on top of onions.

Mix beer, mustard, and caraway seeds in small bowl.
Pour into cooking pot. Cover and cook on Slow Cook
function, Low setting, until bratwursts are tender, about 8
hours, or on High for 4 hours.

Transfer bratwursts to platter. Stir sauerkraut into onion mixture
in cooking pot and let sit until warmed through, about 5 minutes.
Strain onion-sauerkraut mixture through colander, discarding liquid.

Serve bratwursts on rolls, topped with onion-sauerkraut mixture and
mustard.

Beer Brats

Chicken and Dumplings

Chicken and Dumplings

3 pounds boneless, skinless chicken thighs, trimmed and cut into 1-inch pieces

½ teaspoon salt

½ teaspoon pepper

2 Tablespoons olive oil

2 onions, chopped

2 celery stalks, sliced ¼-inch thick

2 carrots, peeled, cut into ¼-inch-thick pieces

4 cloves garlic, minced

1 Tablespoon tomato paste

2 bay leaves

1 teaspoon thyme

¼ cup flour

½ cup white wine

2 cups chicken broth

2 cups vegetable broth

1 cup frozen peas

Dumplings

1¾ cups all-purpose flour

1 Tablespoon baking powder

1 teaspoon salt

1 cup whole milk

4 Tablespoons butter, melted

In a large bowl, rub chicken with salt, pepper, and 1 tablespoon of oil. Heat cooking pot on Brown/Sauté function. Brown chicken in batches until browned on all sides. Set aside.

Add more 1 tablespoon oil to cooking pot. Add onions, celery, and carrots and cook until soft, about 8-10 minutes. Stir in garlic, tomato paste, bay leaves, and thyme and cook until fragrant and tomato paste is starting to brown, about 2 minutes.

Add flour into the pot, stir until combined, and continue to cook for 2 minutes. Whisk in wine and broth and bring to simmer.

Add chicken back to cooking pot, cover and cook on Slow Cook function, Low setting, until chicken is tender, about 4-6 hours. Remove bay leaves and stir in peas.

Dumplings

To create the dumplings, combine the flour, baking powder, and salt together in large bowl. Stir in milk and melted butter. Using greased Tablespoon measure, scoop dough and drop 12 dumplings around perimeter of stew. Cover and cook until dumplings have doubled in size, about 30-35 minutes.

Garlic Ginger Beef with Broccoli

1½ pounds boneless beef chuck roast, well
  trimmed and sliced into thin strips

1 teaspoon olive oil

1 onion, finely chopped

4 garlic

¾ cup beef broth

½ cup soy sauce

⅓ cup brown sugar

3 Tablespoons sesame oil

½ teaspoon red pepper flakes

1 pound broccoli florets

4 Tablespoons water

4 Tablespoons cornstarch

Season beef with salt and pepper. Heat oil
in the cooking pot on Brown/Sauté function.
When oil begins to sizzle, brown meat in
batches until all meat is browned. Transfer
meat to a plate when browned.

Add chopped onion, sauté 1–2 minutes until
onion starts to soften. Add garlic and stir for 1
minute more.

Add beef broth, soy sauce, brown sugar, sesame oil,
and red pepper flakes to the pot. Stir and heat for
another 2 minutes. Add browned beef and juices to
the pot.

Cover and cook on Slow Cook function, Low setting for
about 4 hours.

Place broccoli in microwave-safe bowl with ¼ cup water.
Microwave 3–4 minutes until broccoli is tender.

In a cup combine cornstarch and water; stir until smooth.
Select Brown/Sauté function and add cornstarch mix to
cooking pot. Stir well to combine until sauce comes to a boil
and thickens. Add the broccoli.

Serve over hot cooked rice.

Garlic Ginger Beef with Broccoli

5 Spice Pork Roast

1½ teaspoons salt

1½ teaspoons five-spice powder

½ teaspoon pepper

1 boneless pork tenderloin roast,
 sliced into 1-inch steaks

½ cup hoisin sauce

½ cup honey

½ cup sugar

⅓ cup soy sauce

¼ cup ketchup

2 Tablespoons dry sherry

1 Tablespoon toasted
 sesame oil

1 Tablespoon fresh
 ginger, grated

2 garlic cloves, minced

In a small bowl, combine salt, ¾ teaspoon five-spice powder, and pepper. Rub spice mixture all over pork. In the cooking pot, on Brown/Sauté function, brown the pork roast on all sides.

Cover and cook on Slow Cook function, Low setting, until pork is just tender, about 5–6 hours.

Combine hoisin, honey, sugar, soy sauce, ketchup, sherry, sesame oil, ginger, garlic, and the remaining ¾ teaspoon five-spice powder in a bowl.

In your oven, adjust oven rack 4 inches from broiler element and heat broiler. Line a baking sheet with foil.

Using tongs, transfer pork from cooking pot to foil lined baking sheet. Brush pork with one half of hoisin mixture and broil until lightly caramelized, about 5–7 minutes.

Turn pork over and brush with other half of remaining hoisin mixture, broil until lightly caramelized on second side, about 5–7 minutes.

Slice crosswise into 1-inch steaks and serve.

5 Spice Pork Roast

Jambalaya

Jambalaya

6 boneless chicken thighs, skin removed

4 ounces Andouille sausage, sliced ½ inch thick

2 green bell peppers, chopped

2 celery stalks, sliced

1 bunch scallions, chopped

1 (28-ounce) can diced tomatoes

1 cup long-grain rice

1½ cups chicken broth

2 teaspoons cajun seasoning

2 bay leaves

½ teaspoon dried thyme

⅛ teaspoon cayenne pepper

1 pound large shrimp, peeled and deveined

chopped fresh parsley

In cooking pot, brown the chicken thighs on Brown/Sauté function. Add to the pot the sausage, peppers, celery, scallions, tomatoes, rice, chicken broth, cajun seasoning, bay leaves, thyme, and cayenne pepper.

Cover and cook on Slow Cook function, Low setting, for 4 hours, adding the shrimp during the last 20 minutes of cooking. Discard the bay leaves. Serve topped with parsley.

Chicken Cacciatore

4 bone-in, skin-on chicken legs or thighs

1 Tablespoon vegetable oil

1 pound cremini mushrooms, quartered

1 onion, chopped

4 cloves garlic, minced

2 teaspoons dried oregano

½ teaspoon red pepper flakes

¼ cup tomato paste

1 (28-ounce) can diced tomatoes, drained

½ cup red wine

¼ ounce dried porcini mushrooms, rinsed and patted dry

4 split bone-in chicken breasts, skinless

½ cup fresh basil, chopped

1 Tablespoon red wine vinegar

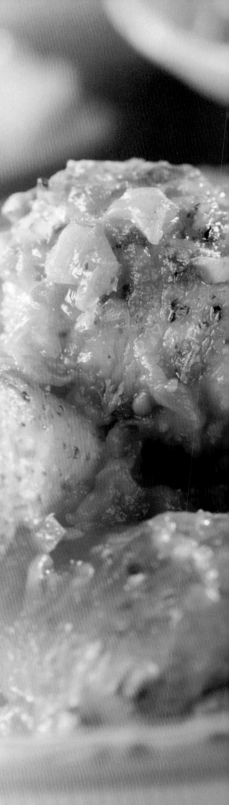

In cooking pot, heat oil on the Brown/Sauté function. Season the legs and thighs with salt and pepper to taste. Brown the meat in cooking pot in batches, then transfer to a plate. Let cool slightly and discard skins.

Pour off and discard all but 1 tablespoon fat from cooking pot. Sauté the cremini mushrooms and onion until golden brown, about 8 minutes. Stir in garlic, oregano, and pepper flakes and cook until fragrant, about 30 seconds. Remove from pot and set aside in a small bowl.

Add tomato paste and ½ can of diced tomatoes to cooking pot and continue to cook until deep red and dry, about 3 minutes. Stir in wine and porcini mushrooms and simmer until liquid is thickened and porcini are softened, about 2 minutes. Add the cremini mixture back into pot.

Place chicken breasts, legs, and thighs into cooking pot and stir to coat chicken with sauce. Cook on Slow Cook function, Low setting, for 4 hours until cooked through.

Remove the chicken and set aside. Stir remaining ½ can tomatoes, basil, and vinegar into sauce. Warm through and spoon sauce over chicken to serve.

Chicken Cacciatore

Corned Beef and Cabbage

Corned Beef and Cabbage

1½ pounds small red skin potatoes, halved

4 carrots, cut into 2-inch pieces

1 large onion, cut into ½-inch wedges

2 stalks celery, peeled and cut into 2-inch pieces

2 or 3 sprigs fresh thyme

4 pounds corned beef, rinsed

12 ounces stout beer or vegetable stock

2 Tablespoons pickling spices

½ small head green cabbage, core intact and cut into thick wedges

1 Tablespoon butter

Layer the potatoes, carrots, onion, celery, and thyme in the cooking pot. Put the brisket on top of the vegetables.

Add the beer (or vegetable stock), spices, and enough water to just cover the brisket. Cover and cook on Slow Cook function, Low setting, until the meat and vegetables are tender, about 8 hours.

Arrange the cabbage over the brisket, cover, and cook until soft and wilted, about 45 minutes to 1 hour more.

Remove the cabbage and, in a large bowl, toss with 1 tablespoon of the butter. Remove the meat and strain the remaining vegetables.

Slice the corned beef against the grain and serve with the vegetables and cabbage.

Asian Chicken Lettuce Wraps

2 pounds ground chicken

3 cloves garlic, minced

1 red bell pepper, finely chopped

½ cup onion, chopped

½ cup hoisin sauce

2 Tablespoons soy sauce

½ teaspoon salt

½ teaspoon black pepper

1 (8-ounce) can water chestnuts, drained and rinsed

1½ cups brown rice, cooked

3 scallions, sliced

1 Tablespoon rice vinegar

1 Tablespoon sesame oil

2 heads Boston or butter lettuce

Place ground chicken and garlic in the cooking pot on Brown/Sauté function. Cook, stirring occasionally, until chicken is no longer pink, about 5-6 minutes. Drain off liquid.

Add bell pepper, onion, hoisin sauce, soy sauce, and salt and pepper and toss the mixture. Cover and cook on Slow Cook function, Low setting, for about 2-3 hours, until chicken is tender.

Stir in water chestnuts, cooked rice, scallions, rice vinegar, and sesame oil and cook until heated through, 3-5 minutes. Season with additional salt as desired.

Separate Boston or butter lettuce leaves. Fill with a few tablespoons of the chicken mixture.

*We like to use ground whole chicken, not just breast, for a juicer wrap.

Asian Chicken Lettuce Wraps

Korean Baby Back Ribs

Pictured above: Todd English

Korean Baby Back Ribs

1 Tablespoon vegetable oil

3 pounds boneless short ribs

2 Tablespoons chile bean paste

4 cloves garlic

4 Tablespoons ginger, grated

¼ teaspoon black pepper

1 cup beef broth

¼ cup soy sauce

2 Tablespoons apple juice

1 Tablespoon rice vinegar

2 Tablespoons brown sugar

1 teaspoon toasted sesame oil

Heat the cooking pot on Brown/Sauté function. Add the oil and cook the short ribs in batches until brown. Set aside on plate.

In large bowl, combine the chile paste, garlic, ginger, and black pepper. Rub onto all sides of meat.

Return meat to the cooking pot and add the broth, soy sauce, apple juice, rice vinegar, brown sugar, and sesame oil.

Set on Slow Cook function, Low setting, and cook for 6-7 hours, or on High for 3-4 hours.

Serve warm.

Chicken Tamales

30 dried cornhusks

1 (2–2½ pound) rotisserie chicken

1 cup red salsa

1 cup green salsa

3 cups masa harina (corn tortilla flour)

½ cup vegetable oil

¾ teaspoon salt

½ teaspoon baking powder

1¾–2 cups chicken broth

10 ounces shredded Monterey Jack cheese

In a bowl, add cornhusks and cover with boiling water. You will need the cornhusks to stay submerged, so use a weighty plate or pot lid to keep the husks under water. Let husks sit for about 30 minutes or until soft and pliable. Drain water and pat dry.

Using two forks, pull chicken from the bone, and shred in a bowl. Mix in both salsas.

In separate bowl add masa harina, oil, salt, baking power and, with electric mixer on medium speed, blend, gradually adding broth until a light, fluffy dough is formed.

Lay a cornhusk flat. On each narrow side of husk, about 1-inch from edge, spread 2 tablespoons of the dough mix, forming a 3×4-inch rectangle. Along the center of rectangle, spoon 2 tablespoons of chicken mix. Sprinkle 1 tablespoon of cheese on top. Fold the long edge of husk over the filling, slightly overlapping the dough. Roll husk around the dough. Using strips of cornhusk, tie ends securely (you can also use kitchen string). Repeat steps for all husks.

In bottom of cooking pot, place a rack or crumpled-up foil. Fill pot with 1-inch water. Tightly stack tamales on rack. Cover and cook on Slow Cook function, High setting, for about 4 hours, or until dough easily pulls away from husk.

Chicken Tamales

Chicken Mole

4 pounds boneless, skinless chicken thighs

1 (28-ounce) can whole tomatoes

1 onion, roughly chopped

2 dried ancho chiles, stems removed

1 large chipotle chile in adobo sauce

½ cup almonds, sliced and toasted

¼ cup raisins

3 ounces bittersweet chocolate, finely chopped

3 garlic cloves, smashed and peeled

3 Tablespoons olive oil

¾ teaspoon ground cumin

½ teaspoon ground cinnamon

fresh cilantro leaves for serving

In the cooking pot, brown chicken in batches until golden brown on each side on Brown/Sauté function.

In a blender, puree tomatoes, onion, ancho and chipotle chiles, almonds, raisins, chocolate, garlic, olive oil, cumin, and cinnamon until smooth.

Add tomato mixture to cooking pot with chicken. Cover and cook on Slow Cook function, High setting, until chicken is tender, about 4 hours, or on Low for 8 hours.

Serve chicken with rice pilaf and sauce topped with cilantro.

Teriyaki Chicken

8 chicken legs, thighs attached

3 Tablespoons cornstarch

1 Tablespoon olive oil

1 bottle teriyaki sauce

3 Tablespoons ginger, grated

3 cloves garlic, grated

3 Tablespoons honey

In a large bowl, dust the chicken legs with cornstarch and season with salt and pepper.

Heat the cooking pot on Brown/Sauté function with 1 tablespoon olive oil. Brown the chicken in batches.

Add the teriyaki sauce, ginger, garlic, honey. Cover and cook on Slow Cook function, Low setting, for 5 hours, or High for 2½ hours.

Serve with Cucumber and Carrot Rice.

Cucumber and Carrot Rice

2 cups rice

3½ cups water

3 Tablespoons olive oil

6 scallions, sliced

1 Tablespoon sesame seeds

1 red bell pepper, cut into thin matchsticks

1 cucumber, cut into thin matchsticks

1 large carrot, cut into thin matchsticks

3 Tablespoons cilantro, roughly chopped

½ lime, freshly juiced

In a medium size pot on stove top, bring water and 2 tablespoons olive oil to a boil. Add rice. Bring the pot of rice to a boil, then reduce to a simmer. Cover and cook for 10-15 minutes until rice is no longer hard. Add additional water if needed. When the rice is done, fluff with a fork.

In a bowl, mix together the scallions, sesame seeds, bell pepper, cucumber, carrot, cilantro, lime juice, and salt and pepper to taste, with 1 tablespoon olive oil. Fold in the cooked rice.

Serve with Teriyaki Chicken.

Coriander Pork Roast

Coriander Pork Roast

1½ teaspoons ground coriander

½ teaspoon red pepper flakes

¼ cup fresh sage

1 Tablespoon fresh flat leaf parsley

1 Tablespoon fresh thyme

1 teaspoon fresh rosemary

1 bay leaf

3 cloves garlic

7 pounds pork shoulder roast

½ cup orange juice

½ cup lemon juice

½ cup chicken broth

½ cup vegetable broth

2 pounds baby red potatoes

1 (14½-ounce) can diced tomatoes

1½ teaspoons sugar

1 cup fresh peppermint

Combine the coriander, red pepper flakes, sage, parsley, thyme, rosemary, bay leaf, garlic, and salt and pepper to taste in a food processor and pulse to make a paste.

Rub the spice paste all over the pork roast. Set into the cooking pot and top with remaining spice paste.

Add a ¼ cup each of orange and lemon juices, broths and potatoes. Cover and cook on Slow Cook function, High setting, for 7½ hours.

Transfer the meat to a cutting board.

Add the tomatoes, sugar and the remaining orange and lemon juice to the cooking pot; cover and cook on Brown/Sauté function for 20 minutes. Stir in the mint just before serving.

Remove the twine from the pork and slice. Serve with the vegetables and the cooking sauce.

Braised Beef Short Ribs

4 (8-ounce) pieces bone-in beef short ribs

1 Tablespoon vegetable oil

¾ teaspoon salt

½ teaspoon black pepper

4 medium carrots, finely chopped

1 medium onion, finely chopped

2 garlic cloves, finely chopped

1 (14-ounce) can whole tomatoes in juice, puréed in a blender with juice

1½ cups dry red wine

4 cups beef stock

2 sprigs fresh thyme

1 Turkish or ½ California bay leaf

1 Tablespoon red wine vinegar

Pat beef dry. Heat oil in a cooking pot on Brown/Sauté function until hot. Brown beef on all sides, about 8 minutes.

Transfer beef to a plate and sprinkle with ¼ teaspoon salt and ¼ teaspoon pepper.

Add to the cooking pot chopped carrots, onion, garlic, tomatoes, wine, stock, thyme, bay leaf, vinegar, and remaining salt and pepper and stir to combine. Return meat to cooking pot and cook on Slow Cook function, High setting for 4–5 hours.

Remove the beef and set aside. Strain sauce and then return the liquids to the cooking pot. Cook on Brown/Sauté function until sauce is reduced by half. Add beef back to pot and coat in the sauce.

Braised Beef Short Ribs

Lamb Shanks with Potatoes

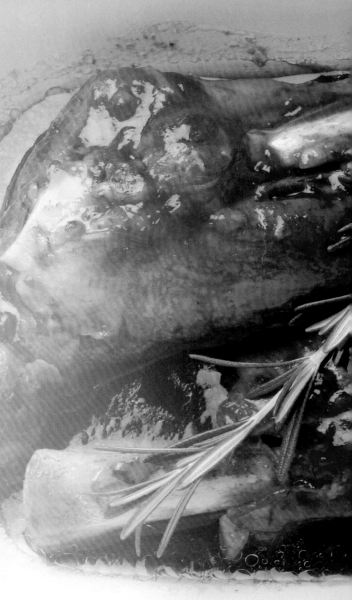

3½ pounds lamb shanks, cut crosswise into 1½-inch pieces and trimmed of excess fat

4 Tablespoons flour

2 Tablespoons olive oil

½ cup white wine

1¼ pounds red potatoes

4 shallots, cut into ¼-inch wedges

3 garlic cloves, thinly sliced

1 Tablespoon lemon zest, grated, plus 2 Tablespoons lemon juice

3 sprigs rosemary

¾ cup chicken broth

Season lamb with salt and pepper to taste, then coat in 3 tablespoons of flour, shaking off excess.

In a cooking pot, heat oil on Brown/Sauté function. In batches, cook lamb until browned on all sides.

Add wine to the cooking pot and continue to cook on Brown/Sauté function, stirring until reduced by half, about 2 minutes.

Add potatoes, shallots, garlic, lemon zest, rosemary, 1 tablespoon flour, and broth to wine in cooking pot. Return lamb to cooking pot.

Cook on Slow Cook function, High setting, until lamb is tender, about 3½ hours or Low for 7 hours.

Lamb Shanks with Potatoes

Cuban Pork Sandwiches

2 Tablespoons extra-virgin olive oil

1 Tablespoon salt

2 teaspoons ground cumin

2 teaspoons oregano

1 teaspoon ground black pepper

¼ teaspoon crushed red pepper

3-4 cloves garlic, minced

2 Tablespoons lime juice

2 Tablespoons orange juice

3½ pounds boneless pork shoulder

8-inch sub rolls

yellow mustard

1 pound Swiss cheese, thick sliced

1 pound ham, thinly sliced

2 cups dill pickle chips

2 red onions, thinly sliced

Mix the oil, salt, cumin, oregano, black pepper, red pepper, garlic, lime juice, and orange juice in a small bowl.

Coat the pork in the spice rub. Place the pork in the cooking pot and add the remaining juices from the bowl.

Cover and cook on Slow Cook function, Low setting, for 3 hours. Turn over meat and cook for 3 more hours.

Remove pork from the cooking pot and let cool slightly. Shred the pork into thick chunks.

Slice the sub rolls open and layer with the mustard, Swiss cheese, ham, pulled pork, pickles, and onion slices.

Korean Beef Tacos

5 pounds beef chuck roast

10 ounces soy sauce

1 cup brown sugar

6 cloves garlic, minced

4 Tablespoons fresh ginger, grated

6 Tablespoons rice vinegar

2 Tablespoons dark sesame oil

2 Tablespoons olive oil

2 Tablespoons sriracha

1 cup water

16 small corn tortillas

fresh cilantro, chopped

bean sprouts

sour cream

sriracha

In a small bowl, whisk soy sauce, sugar, garlic, ginger, vinegar, oils, sriracha, and water. Place the beef in the cooking pot and pour the soy mix over meat. Cook on Slow Cook function, Low setting, for 8 hours.

Remove beef from pot and let cool slightly. While beef is cooling, switch to Brown/Sauté function and cook the liquid down by half. Shred the beef and add back into the reduced liquid in cooking pot.

Assemble your tacos by placing the beef on corn tortillas.

Serve with toppings as desired and with Cucumber Salad.

Cucumber Salad

2 cucumbers, seeds removed

1 red onion, thinly sliced

1 teaspoon salt

4 Tablespoons rice vinegar

red pepper flakes to taste

Slice the cucumber very thinly and sprinkle with salt. Place in a colander and let sit for up to an hour over a bowl or in the sink.

Rinse cucumbers off with cold water. Shake additional water from the colander.

Transfer to a bowl and toss with red onion, rice vinegar, and red pepper flakes.

Refrigerate until ready to use.

Serve with Korean Beef Tacos.

Buffalo Pulled Chicken Sandwiches

1 Tablespoon olive oil

1 pound boneless, skinless chicken thighs, cut into 1½-inch pieces

1 pound boneless, skinless chicken breast, cut into 1½-inch pieces

1 yellow onion, finely diced

3 garlic cloves, roughly chopped

1 red bell pepper, seeded and finely diced

1 (14.5-ounce) can crushed tomatoes

¼ cup hot sauce

3 Tablespoons Worcestershire sauce

2 Tablespoons mustard

1 Tablespoon molasses

8 hamburger buns

In cooking pot, heat oil on Brown/Sauté function. Add chicken thighs, season with salt and pepper to taste, and brown. Transfer to a plate and repeat with the breast meat.

In the cooking pot, add onion, garlic, and bell pepper; cook until onion is translucent, about 6 minutes.

Add browned chicken, crushed tomatoes, hot pepper sauce, Worcestershire, mustard, and molasses; stir to combine.

Cover and cook on Slow Cook function, High setting, for 4 hours. Shred chicken and season to taste with salt and pepper. Serve on buns.

Buffalo Pulled Chicken Sandwiches

Meatball-Sausage Subs

Meatball-Sausage Subs

2 (28-ounce) cans tomatoes, crushed by hand

1 (6-ounce) can tomato paste

2 bay leaves

½ teaspoon salt

½ teaspoon pepper

1½ cups Parmesan cheese, grated, plus 1 small piece Parmesan rind

1 cup water

¼ cup parsley, chopped

2 cloves garlic, chopped

¾ cup breadcrumbs

½ cup whole milk

1½ pounds ground beef chuck

2 large eggs

½ cup parsley, chopped

2 cloves garlic, chopped

1 teaspoon salt

½ teaspoon pepper

1½ pounds sweet and/or hot Italian sausages , cut into 1-inch pieces

2 loaves French bread, cut into 3-inch slices and split open

mozzarella cheese, shredded, for topping

In cooking pot combine the crushed tomatoes, tomato paste, bay leaves, salt, pepper, Parmesan rind, water, parsley, and garlic cloves. Set aside.

Combine the breadcrumbs and milk in a medium bowl; soak 2 minutes.

In a separate bowl, combine the beef, eggs, 1 cup Parmesan, the remaining ¼ cup parsley and 2 garlic cloves, and salt and pepper.

Add in the breadcrumb-milk mixture and mix until combined. Shape into 24 meatballs, about 1½ inches in diameter; gently set in prepared sauce in cooking pot.

Add the sausage pieces to the cooking pot, cover and cook on Slow Cook function, Low setting, for 7 hours. Remove the bay leaves and Parmesan rind and stir in the remaining ½ cup Parmesan. Serve on the sliced bread and top with the mozzarella cheese.

Picnic Ham with Barbecue Beans

1 pound dried navy beans

1 onion, chopped

½ cup ketchup

¼ cup maple syrup

¼ cup packed dark brown sugar

2 Tablespoons mustard

1½ Tablespoons dark molasses

2 teaspoons Worcestershire sauce

1 teaspoon apple cider vinegar

4–7 pounds bone-in ham

Combine beans, 3 cups water, onion, ketchup, maple syrup, brown sugar, mustard, molasses, Worcestershire sauce, and vinegar in cooking pot. Set the ham on top, then cover and cook on Slow Cook function, High setting, for 8 hours.

Transfer the ham to a platter and skim off the excess fat from the beans. Slice the ham and serve with the beans.

Picnic Ham with Barbecue Beans

Tex-Mex Casserole

2 (15-ounce) cans refried pinto beans

2 cups frozen corn

2 poblano chili peppers, seeded and chopped

½ cup fresh cilantro, chopped

2 teaspoons ground cumin

1 teaspoon ancho chile powder

1 (16-ounce) jar salsa

1 (10-ounce) can diced tomatoes with green chiles

8 ounces shredded Cheddar cheese

8 ounces shredded Provolone cheese

18–20 corn tostada shells

2 avocados, sliced

sour cream and pickled jalapeños, for topping (optional)

In a medium bowl, combine the refried beans, frozen corn, poblanos, ¼ cup cilantro, cumin, and chile powder. In a separate medium bowl, combine the salsa, tomatoes, and the remaining ¼ cup cilantro. In a third bowl, toss the cheddar and provolone cheese; set aside.

Spread about ½ cup of the salsa mixture in a thin layer on bottom of cooking pot. Top with about 6 tostada shells, breaking them as needed to cover the salsa mixture. Spread half of the bean mixture over the tostada shells, then sprinkle with 1½ cups of the cheese mixture and 1 cup of the salsa mixture.

Repeat the layers (tostada shells, bean mixture, cheese, salsa mixture). Top with the remaining tostadas, cheese and salsa.

Cover and cook on Slow Cook function, Low setting, for 4 hours. Uncover and let rest 15 minutes. Serve with the sliced avocados, sour cream, cilantro, and pickled jalapeños.

Curried Chicken

3 pounds boneless, skinless chicken thighs

2 onions, thinly sliced

8 garlic cloves, thinly sliced

2 ounces fresh ginger, peeled and sliced

2 Tablespoons curry powder

1 teaspoon ground coriander

1 teaspoon ground cumin

1 teaspoon salt

2 (10-ounce) packages frozen peas

2 cups unsweetened coconut milk

½ cup toasted cashews

¼ cup cilantro leaves

Brown chicken in batches in cooking pot on the Brown/Sauté function. When finished, return all the chicken to cooking pot.

Add in the onion, garlic, ginger, curry powder, coriander, cumin, and salt to coat chicken. Cover and cook on Slow Cook function, High setting, for 4 hours.

Stir in peas and coconut milk; cover and cook until peas are heated through, about 20 minutes.

Transfer chicken to a large bowl and shred with fork. Return to pot and toss with the curry sauce.

To serve, garnish with cashews and cilantro leaves.

Lemongrass Halibut

2 garlic cloves, smashed
1 stalk lemongrass, quartered
1 shallot, thinly sliced
1 stalk celery, sliced
1-inch piece ginger, thinly sliced
1–1¼ pounds fresh halibut
1 Tablespoon extra-virgin olive oil

In cooking pot place garlic, lemongrass, shallot, celery, and ginger. Place fish on top of vegetables.

On top of fish, drizzle the extra-virgin olive oil. Season with salt and pepper to taste.

Cook on Slow Cook function, High setting, for 1–1½ hours or until fish flakes apart.

Lemongrass Halibut

French Dip Sandwiches

French Dip Sandwiches

3 scallions
2 teaspoons fresh thyme
1 clove garlic, crushed
1 teaspoon salt
1 teaspoon pepper
¼ teaspoon celery seeds
¼ teaspoon ground allspice
1½ pounds beef eye round roast
2 carrots, sliced 1-inch thick
2 Tablespoons Worcestershire sauce
1½ cups of beef broth
6 French baguette rolls, sliced in half
  lengthwise
creamy horseradish for serving

Pulse the scallions, thyme, garlic, salt, pepper, celery seeds, and allspice in a food processor to make a paste. Rub the spice paste into the meat.

Spread the carrots in cooking pot and set the roast on top. Add broth to cooking pot.

Cover and cook on Slow Cook function, Low setting until the meat registers 120-130 degrees for medium rare, about 2 hours. Transfer the meat to a cutting board and cover with foil; let rest 15 minutes. Skim off the excess fat from the cooking liquid.

Slice the meat very thinly. Spoon some cooking liquid onto the cut sides of each slice of bread; top with the meat and horseradish. Serve with more cooking liquid for dipping.

Ginger Steak

3 pounds beef sirloin

2 Tablespoons olive oil

3 Tablespoons cornstarch

3 cloves garlic, chopped

3 Tablespoons ginger, peeled and cut into fine strips

1 onion, sliced

2 red bell peppers, sliced

2 yellow bell peppers, sliced

2 green bell peppers, sliced

1 (8-ounce) can tomato sauce

4 Tablespoons brown sugar

¾ cup soy sauce

1 cup cilantro, roughly chopped

2 limes, quartered

In the cooking pot, heat the olive oil on Brown/Sauté function. Add sirloin and cook until just browned on both sides. Remove the steak to a cutting board and slice it into 1-inch-thick strips.

Place the sliced steak into the pot, then sprinkle the meat with cornstarch and stir until all in the cornstarch is incorporated.

Add garlic, ginger, onion, peppers, tomato sauce, sugar, and soy sauce to the cooking pot. Cover and cook on Slow Cook function, Low setting, for 6 hours.

Top with cilantro and serve with lime quarters and rice.

Maple Dijon Chicken and Broccoli

⅓ cup pure maple syrup

3 Tablespoons Dijon mustard

1 Tablespoon whole grain mustard

1 Tablespoon red wine vinegar

2 cloves garlic, minced

½ teaspoon dried rosemary

½ teaspoon dried oregano

1 orange zest

8 brown sugar

8 chicken thighs

2 Tablespoons butter

2 heads broccoli, cut into florets

In a medium bowl, whisk together maple syrup, mustards, red wine vinegar, garlic, rosemary, oregano, and orange zest; set aside.

Using your fingers, work the brown sugar onto both sides of the chicken thighs.

In cooking pot on Brown/Sauté function, melt butter and brown chicken, 2–3 minutes per side.

Stir in maple syrup mixture. Cover and cook on Slow Cook function, Low setting, for 5–6 hours, or High for 2–3 hours.

Add broccoli during the last 30 minutes of cooking time.

Wild Mushroom and Brie Cheese Bread Pudding

5 cups French bread, torn into
  ½-inch cubes

½ cup shiitake mushrooms

½ cup morel mushrooms

½ cup chanterelle mushrooms

4 ounces Andouille sausage,
  chopped

½ cup onion, chopped

6 ounces brie cheese, cut into
  ½-inch pieces

4 eggs, lightly beaten

2 cups half and half

1 teaspoon thyme

½ teaspoon rosemary

Combine bread, mushrooms, sausages, onions, and cheese in the cooking pot.

In a bowl combine the eggs, half and half, thyme, and rosemary. Pour over the bread mixture in cooking pot.

Cover and cook on Slow Cook function, Low setting, for 5 hours. Let stand for 15 minutes before serving.

Wild Mushroom and Brie Cheese Bread Pudding

Beef Stroganoff

2 pounds beef chuck roast, cut into thin strips

1 onion, chopped

1 pound button mushrooms, quartered

1½ teaspoons salt

1 teaspoon pepper

2 Tablespoons cornstarch

½ cup sour cream

2 Tablespoons Dijon-style mustard

egg noodles, cooked, for serving

In a cooking pot, toss beef, onion, and mushrooms with 1½ teaspoons salt and 1 teaspoon pepper.

Cover, and cook on Slow Cook function, Low setting, for 8 hours.

In a measuring cup, whisk cornstarch with 2 tablespoons water. Stir cornstarch mixture into the beef until thickened. Add sour cream and mustard.

Serve beef over egg noodles.

Mongolian Beef

1 pound steak, cut into 1-inch pieces

¼ cup cornstarch

2 teaspoons olive oil

1 onion, thinly sliced

1 Tablespoon garlic, chopped

3 scallions, thinly sliced

½ cup soy sauce

½ cup water

½ cup brown sugar

1 teaspoon ginger, minced

½ cup hoisin sauce

Place flank steak and cornstarch into a resealable plastic bag. Shake the bag to evenly coat the flank steak with the cornstarch.

Heat olive oil in cooking pot on Brown/Sauté function. Stir steak until evenly browned, about 4–6 minutes.

Add to cooking pot, onion, garlic, scallions, soy sauce, water, brown sugar, ginger, and hoisin sauce. Cover and cook on Slow Cook function, Low setting for about 4 hours.

Serve with rice.

Desserts & Beverages

Desserts & Beverages

Pecan Pie

1 pie crust, refrigerated

3 eggs

1 cup sugar

⅔ cup corn syrup

⅓ cup butter, melted

¼ teaspoon salt

1 teaspoon vanilla extract

5½ cups pecans, chopped (or a combination of chopped and whole pecan halves)

vanilla ice cream, for serving

Line the cooking pot with foil. This will make it easier to lift out of the pot.

Place pie crust in the pot and mold it to fit the shape of the cooking pot.

Stir eggs together in bowl with sugar, corn syrup, butter, salt, and vanilla extract until mixed well.

Stir in half of the pecans and leave the other half to arrange on top of the filling, to make it look prettier.

Pour filling into pie crust. Gently place the other half of the pecans on top of the filling.

Cover and set on Slow Cook function, High setting, for 2½–3 hours.

Serve with vanilla ice cream.

Apple Cider

9 apples, assorted types

1 orange

3 cinnamon sticks

1 whole nutmeg

2 teaspoons whole cloves

½ teaspoon whole allspice

16 cups water

2-3 cups brown sugar

Cut the apples and orange into quarters and place into the cooking pot.

Add cinnamon sticks, nutmeg, cloves and allspice. Cover with water, filling the pot until it is about 2 inches from the top.

Cook on Slow Cook function, High setting, for 3-4 hours, or on Low for 6-8 hours. You can add more water if needed during the cooking process.

About an hour before the cider is done cooking, use a potato masher to mash the apple and orange slices. Finish cooking for one more hour.

Strain out the apple cider juice into a clean pitcher or pot. To get the maximum juice out of the apples, you can press them through a fine mesh strainer or strain through a cheesecloth.

Stir in your desired amount of sugar until it is dissolved.

White Chocolate Cranberry Shortbread Bars

2 sticks butter

¾ cup sugar

1 teaspoon vanilla extract

1 egg

¼ teaspoon salt

2 cups flour

4 ounces white chocolate baking bar, chopped (or white chocolate baking chips)

½ cup cranberries

Line with your cooking pot with foil.

With your mixer beat together butter, sugar, and vanilla. Add the egg and salt and mix until combined. Add flour, a little at a time, and mix until dough forms.

With wooden spoon, stir in white chocolate and cranberries.

Spread dough evenly in bottom of the cooking pot. Cover and set on Slow Cook function, Low setting, for 2-3 hours. Let cool for 30 minutes and lift the foil to remove from cooking pot.

Slice and serve.

Apple Cider

Baked Stuffed Apples

Baked Stuffed Apples

¾ cup walnuts, toasted and chopped

½ cup dried cranberries, chopped

⅓ cup packed light brown sugar

⅓ cup rolled oats

3 Tablespoons butter, cut into small pieces

1 Tablespoon fresh lemon juice

½ teaspoon ground cinnamon

½ teaspoon salt

4 large or 6 medium firm baking apples (such as Rome, Golden delicious, or Honey crisp)

1 cup apple cider

vanilla ice cream and pure maple syrup for serving

Combine the walnuts, cranberries, brown sugar, oats, butter, lemon juice, cinnamon, and ½ teaspoon salt in a small bowl and squeeze together until a wet and sandy mixture is formed.

Scoop the core out of each apple with a melon baller, taking care not to scoop completely through to the bottom or the sides.

Stuff each apple with some of the cranberry-walnut mixture. Place the apples in the cooking pot and pour in the apple cider.

Cover and set on Slow Cook function, Low setting, for 3–4, hours or until the apples are tender but still slightly firm. Depending on the size and type of apple, check after 2 hours, as smaller apples may cook faster.

Serve each apple whole or cut in half with a scoop of ice cream and a drizzle of the pure maple syrup.

Vanilla Latte

8 cups whole milk
4 cups coffee, double strength

1 cup vanilla coffee liqueur
whipped cream

In the cooking pot, add milk, coffee, and vanilla coffee liqueur. Stir until combined.

Heat it on Slow Cook function, Low setting, until heated through, about 2 hours.

Ladle latte mix into individual mugs. Top with whipped cream and serve.

(Keep leftovers in the refrigerator and use as iced coffee.)

Cinnamon Sugar Candied Almonds

1½ cups sugar

1½ cups light brown sugar

3 Tablespoons ground cinnamon

⅛ teaspoon salt

1 egg white

2 teaspoons vanilla

4½ cups raw almonds

¼ cup water

Spray your cooking pot with nonstick spray and set aside.

In a large bowl, add the sugar, brown sugar, cinnamon, and salt. Whisk together. In another large bowl, add the egg white and vanilla and whisk until frothy. Pour the almonds in the egg mixture and toss them around to coat thoroughly. Pour the coated almonds into the sugar mixture and toss to coat.

Pour the entire mixture into the cooking pot and set on Slow Cook function, Low setting. Cook for 3–3½ hours, stirring every 20 minutes. It will look like not much is happening for a long time but your house will smell good!

After 3 hours, pour in the ¼ cup of water and stir well. This is going to make the crunchy coating and things will start looking right. Leave in the cooking pot for another 20–30 minutes.

Meanwhile, line a baking sheet with parchment paper.

When done, pour the almonds onto the prepared baking sheet and separate any that stuck together. Let them cool slightly to harden then enjoy!

Banana Upside Down Cake

Banana Upside Down Cake

5 Tablespoons unsalted butter

¾ cup firmly packed dark brown sugar

3 Tablespoons dark rum

2 pounds ripe medium bananas, peeled and halved lengthwise

¾ cup cake flour

¾ teaspoon baking powder

½ teaspoon ground cinnamon

¼ teaspoon ground nutmeg

¼ teaspoon salt

4 Tablespoons butter, room temperature

⅔ cup sugar

1 egg

1 egg yolk

2 Tablespoons whole milk

ice cream for serving

Butter the inside of the cooking pot, line completely with foil, and then butter the foil. Heat the cooking pot on Brown/Sauté function.

Sprinkle butter, brown sugar, and rum over the foil on the bottom. Cover the bottom with the banana halves, cut-side down, in a slightly overlapping pattern. Press the bananas into the sugar.

Whisk together the flour, baking powder, cinnamon, nutmeg, and salt in a large bowl.

In another bowl, slowly beat the butter and sugar with an electric mixer on low, until just blended. Raise the speed to high and beat until light and fluffy, scraping the sides of the bowl occasionally, about 10 minutes.

Beat in the egg and then the yolk, allowing each to be fully incorporated before adding the next.

While mixing slowly, add the flour mixture to the butter in 3 parts, alternating with the milk in 2 parts, beginning and ending with the flour. Mix at medium speed to make a smooth batter.

Pour the batter over the bananas and smooth with a spatula to even it out. Lay a doubled length of paper towel from end to end over the top of the cooking pot to line the lid. This is an important step to catch condensation and allow the cake to cook.

Cover the cake tightly with the lid and continue to cook on Slow Cook function, High setting, until the cake begins to brown slightly on the sides and springs back when touched in the middle, about 3½ hours. Turn off the cooker, remove lid, and let the cake set, about 20 minutes more.

Using the foil, lift the cake from the cooker; set on the counter to cool, about 30 minutes more. Fold back the foil, and carefully invert cake onto a platter so you can see the caramelized bananas.

Slice or spoon cake into bowls and serve with ice cream, if desired.

ALLISON WAGGONER

Lemon Cookie Bars

1½ sticks butter, room temperature

½ cup sugar

1 teaspoon vanilla extract

¼ teaspoon salt

1 egg

2 cups all-purpose flour

1 (10-ounce) jar lemon curd

¼ cup powdered sugar

In large bowl beat together butter, sugar, vanilla, and salt (I used my handheld mixer).

Add in the egg and mix until combined. Slowly add flour and continue to mix until dough forms.

Press dough evenly in the bottom of the cooking pot. Evenly spread lemon curd over the top of the dough.

Cover and set on Slow Cook function, High setting, for 2-4 hours.

Let cool in the pot. Cut into squares and remove.

Dust with powdered sugar using sifter or fine mesh strainer. Serve or store in airtight container.

Peach Cobbler

6 ounces dark brown sugar

3½ ounces rolled oats

4 ounces all-purpose flour

½ teaspoon baking powder

½ teaspoon ground allspice

½ teaspoon nutmeg, freshly grated

¼ teaspoon salt

¼ cup unsalted butter, room temperature, plus extra for the cooker

1 (20-ounce) package frozen peaches, sliced

Combine the sugar, oats, flour, baking powder, allspice, nutmeg, and salt in a large bowl. Add the butter and work into the dry ingredients until a crumbly texture is formed. Fold in the peach slices.

Butter the bottom and sides of your cooking pot. Add the mixture to the pot and set on Slow Cook function, Low setting, for 3–3½ hours. Serve immediately.

Peach Cobbler

Hot Fudge Cake

1 Tablespoon butter, room temperature,
  for greasing

1½ sticks butter, melted

3 eggs

1½ cups sugar

⅔ cup unsweetened cocoa powder

⅓ cup all-purpose flour

1 teaspoon vanilla extract

½ teaspoon salt

½ cup semisweet chocolate, broken into
  pieces

vanilla ice cream

Line the cooking pot with a piece of foil,
then grease the foil with 1 tablespoon of
butter. Set aside.

Slightly beat the eggs until mixed
together. In a separate bowl, stir together
the melted butter, sugar, cocoa powder,
flour, beaten eggs, vanilla, and ½ teaspoon
salt. Sprinkle in the chocolate chunks and
stir until chocolate is just mixed into the
batter.

Transfer the batter into the foil-lined
cooker pot. Cover and set to Slow Cook
function, Low setting for 3 hours; the
cake should be set around the edges and
gooey in the center.

Serve the cake warm, spooned into a
bowl, and topped with ice cream.

Hot Fudge Cake

Sour Cream Cheesecake

¾ cup graham cracker crumbs

2½ Tablespoons butter, melted

¼ teaspoon ground cinnamon

⅔ cup plus 1 Tablespoon sugar

¼ teaspoon salt

1 (12-ounce) package cream cheese, room temperature

1 Tablespoon all-purpose flour

2 eggs

1 teaspoon almond extract

1 cup sour cream

In a medium bowl, mix the graham cracker crumbs with the melted butter, cinnamon, 1 tablespoon of the sugar, and a pinch of salt. Press the crumbs over the bottom and 1 inch up the sides of a 6-inch springform pan that is 3 inches deep. (Use a pan that will fit into your multicooker.)

With a mixer, combine the cream cheese with the flour, the remaining ⅔ cup of sugar and ¼ teaspoon of salt. Beat at medium-high speed until smooth, about 2 minutes. Add the eggs and the almond extract. Mix the sour cream mix until smooth. Pour the batter into the springform pan.

Fill your cooking pot with ½ inch of water and position a rack or crumpled foil in the bottom. Set the cheesecake on the rack above water. Cover the top of the cooking pot with a triple layer of paper towels and cover with the lid. Set the cooker on Slow Cook function, High setting, and cook for 2 hours.

Turn off the heat and let stand until the cooker has cooled, about 1 hour.

Refrigerate until chilled, at least 4 hours.

Cut into wedges and serve.

Chai Tea

3½ quarts water

15 slices fresh ginger, peeled and sliced

15 cardamom pods, split open and seeded

25 whole cloves

3 cinnamon sticks

3 whole black peppercorns

3 star anise

8 black teabags

Pour water into the cooking pot. Stir in the ginger, cardamom pods, cloves, cinnamon sticks, peppercorns, and star anise

Turn to Slow Cook function, High setting, and simmer for 8 hours.

Place tea bags in the hot, spiced water and steep for 5 minutes. Strain tea into a clean container.

Stir in sweetened condensed milk; serve hot.

Chocolate-Hazelnut Bread Pudding

Chocolate-Hazelnut Bread Pudding

1 (14-ounce) package brioche bread, cut into 1-inch cubes (12 cups)

2 cups heavy cream

2 cups whole milk

9 egg yolks

1 cup Nutella

¾ cup plus 1 Tablespoon sugar

4 teaspoons vanilla extract

¾ teaspoon salt

½ cup chocolate chips

2 Tablespoons light brown sugar

Adjust oven rack to middle position and heat oven to 225 degrees. Spread bread over rimmed baking sheet and spray with vegetable oil. Bake, shaking pan occasionally, until bread is dry and crisp, about 40 minutes. Let bread cool slightly.

In cooking pot, whisk the cream, milk, egg yolks, Nutella, ¾ cup sugar, vanilla, and salt together. Add in the chocolate chips and cooled dried bread and toss to coat everything together. Press gently on the bread to submerge it.

Mix the remaining tablespoon of sugar with brown sugar, then sprinkle over the top.

Cover and cook on Slow Cook function, Low setting, until center is set, about 4 hours. Let cool for 30 minutes before serving.

Key Lime Pie

Crust

¾ cup graham cracker crumbs

4 Tablespoons unsalted butter, melted

1 Tablespoon sugar

Filling

4 large egg yolks

1 (14-ounce) can sweetened condensed milk

½ cup key lime juice, freshly squeezed

⅓ cup sour cream

2 Tablespoons key lime zest, grated

Crust

In a small 1-quart pyrex glass bowl that will fit inside your cooking pot (or you can use individual silicone cups), combine the graham cracker crumbs, butter, and sugar. Press evenly in the bottom and up the sides of the pan. Place in the freezer for 10 minutes.

Filling

In a large mixing bowl, beat the egg yolks until they are light yellow. Gradually beat in sweetened condensed milk until thickened. Gradually add lime juice and beat until smooth. Stir in sour cream and zest. Pour batter into the baking dish on top of the crust. Cover top of dish with aluminum foil.

Fill your cooking pot with ½ inch of water and position a rack in the bottom. Set the pan on the rack above water. Cover the top of the cooking pot with a triple layer of paper towels and cover with the lid. Set the cooker on Slow Cook function, High setting, and cook for 2 hours.

Turn off the heat and let stand until the cooker has cooled, about 1 hour.

Key Lime Pie

Mexican Hot Chocolate

8 Tablespoons cocoa powder, unsweetened

2 cups hot water

12 ounces bittersweet chocolate

2 (7-ounce) cans sweetened condensed milk

4 cinnamon sticks

2 teaspoons ground cinnamon

1 teaspoon nutmeg

1 teaspoon chili powder

12 cups whole milk

In the cooking pot, combine the hot water and the cocoa powder; stir until smooth.

Add the bittersweet chocolate, condensed milk, cinnamon sticks, cinnamon, nutmeg, chili powder, and whole milk.

Heat on Slow Cooker function, Low setting, for 2 hours, stirring every 30 minutes.

Serve warm with marshmallows, whipped cream, chocolate syrup, or chocolate shavings.

Mexican Hot Chocolate

Lavender Pear Cake

Lavender Pear Cake

2 cups almond flour

½ cup all-purpose flour

1 teaspoon baking powder

½ teaspoon salt

1 teaspoon vanilla extract

2 eggs

¼ cup milk

9 tablespoons butter, melted

4 tablespoons corn syrup

2 medium pears, cut into ½ -inch pieces

1 teaspoon dried ground lavender

Line the cooking pot with foil or liner.

In a large bowl, mix the almond flour, flour, baking powder, salt. Combine well.

In a separate small bowl, add in the vanilla, eggs, milk, melted butter, and corn syrup. Whisk with a fork until combined. Pour into the dry ingredients and fold through until you form a smooth batter.

Add in the pears and lavender and stir. Place mixture into the lined cooking pot and smooth out the top.

Cover and cook on Slow Cook function, Low setting for 4 hours or High for 2 hours. Check the cake by inserting a toothpick into the center, which should come out clean. If not, continue cooking on High setting with the lid off until cake is cooked.

Rice Pudding

8 cups milk

1 cup long-grain white rice (not instant)

1 cup sugar

¼ cup half and half

2 teaspoons vanilla extract

1 teaspoon ground cinnamon

3 Tablespoons cornstarch

9 Tablespoons water

Combine milk, rice, sugar, and half and half in cooking pot. Stir well, and cook on Slow Cook function, Low setting, for 6–7 hours, or on High for 4–5 hours.

Add in the vanilla, cinnamon, and salt to taste into the mixture.

In a small bowl, mix together water and cornstarch until well combined. Stir cornstarch mix into the rice/spice mixture and cook for another 30 minutes.

Lemon-Poppy Seed Cake

Cake

2 cups all-purpose flour

¼ cup poppy seeds

1 teaspoon baking powder

½ teaspoon salt

1 cup sugar

3 eggs

½ cup vegetable oil

½ cup Greek yogurt

¼ cup milk

1 teaspoon lemon zest

¼ cup fresh lemon juice

1 teaspoon vanilla

Icing

2 cups powdered sugar

½ teaspoon lemon zest

lemon juice and/or milk

Cake

In a large bowl, combine flour, poppy seeds, baking powder, and salt.

In a medium bowl whisk together sugar, eggs, oil, yogurt, milk, lemon zest, lemon juice, and vanilla until sugar dissolves.

Add sugar mixture all at once to flour mixture. Stir just until combined (mixture should still be slightly lumpy). Spoon batter into cooking pot.

Cover and cook on Slow Cook function, High setting, for 1½–2 hours or until top appears set. Turn off cooker and take off lid. Place paper towel inside of cooking pot on top of cake. Completely cover with paper towels; cover with lid. Cool for 10 to 15 minutes. Run a knife around edges of cooking pot then remove bread from cooker.

Icing

Mix the powdered sugar, lemon zest, and just enough lemon juice or milk to create consistency to easily drizzle over cake.

Index

About the Author

Allison Waggoner, acclaimed television host, seen in more than 80 million homes, has recorded more than 80,000 hours of LIVE television, which is more than Oprah and Jay Leno combined! You can see Allison in the kitchen with celebrities, such as Chefs Todd English, Andrew Zimmern, Paula Deen, Bobby Deen, Jamie Deen, Kevin Dundon, the Beekman Boys, and Captain Sig Hanson. You've seen her on The Food Network's *Unwrapped*, and you can currently join in with her on *Evine Live*. Just in case you didn't know her true passion, it's FOOD and sharing it with YOU! As a classically trained chef, Allison's culinary and marketing career brought her to the attention of television executives. She first appeared as a guest host, bringing her confections and family culinary history to the home shopping world.

Growing up in the chocolate industry inspired a journey filled with delicious and innovative cuisine. Allison started with her family's gourmet chocolates, creating some of the finest award-winning confections in the world. Her culinary designs have been featured in Crate & Barrel, Culinary Product Magazine, Ghirardelli Chocolate Company, Godiva Chocolatier, Walt Disney World, Fancy Food Magazine, Target, Universal Studios, Williams-Sonoma, and on The Food Network.

Her In the Kitchen cookbook series began with *A Collection of Home and Family Memories*, released in 2014. Her second book, *A Gathering of Friends*, is a nostalgic collection of recipes to celebrate the moments in our lives and is filled with simple, delicious dishes for every day of the week. Added to her collection is *Air Fryer Cookbook*, the #1 bestselling air fryer book in the country, including a newly released updated edition.

Alison lives in the Twin Cities, Minnesota.

Visit her at www.allisonwaggoner.com

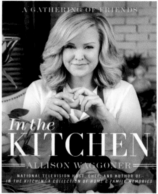
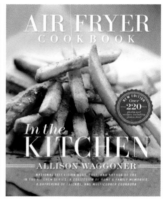

SCAN to visit

www.allisonwaggoner.com

Rosemary

Oregano

Basil

Spinach